CW01210411

This booklet is dedicated to my Father, who would have been delighted that the records of his father's voyages had finally been put together!

Thanks to Doug, who inspired the exercise

Foreword

The author is the grandson of a man called Arthur Newton Owen, who referred to himself as 'Art'. He was born in 1877, and went to sea when he was 16. The life he led for the next ten years was so different than anything I or my brother have done that we thought we'd share it with others.

The key thing, of course, is that we've got enough records to be able to reconstruct what he did and where he went. We have his diaries for most of his voyages, and records of his service on a variety of ships. There is enough, with other sources on the internet, to be able to piece together what life must have been like for him at sea at the end of the Victorian era.

How typical his experience was is difficult to gauge; but in the ten years between his 16th birthday, and becoming licensed as a Thames River pilot (which was the aim of the whole exercise), he went round the world five times and sailed across the Atlantic eleven times. He ended with an 'Extra Master' certificate, which allowed him to be master of almost any size of ship, sailing anywhere in the world.

Why does the story stop in 1903? Because he got the job as a pilot, bought a house, got married, and, as far as we know, never went further away from home than the Isle of Wight for the rest of his life!

And the pea soup? A key part of his diet on the wool clipper 'Mermerus'!

May 2024

Contents

1. Beginnings
2. Seamanship
3. Conditions
4. Setting the Sails
5. Steam ships
6. The brig 'Messenger'
7. The voyage of the 'Peri' to Fremantle.
8. The voyage of the 'Peri': Fremantle to Cape Town
9. The voyage of the 'Peri': Cape Town to London
10. Closer to Home

Appendix 1: Sources for Illustrations

Appendix 2: Further reading

Appendix 3: Glossary

1   Beginnings

My grandfather Arthur Newton Owen was born in 1877, the first child of Arthur Robert and Elizabeth Owen, who had got married the year before. Arthur Newton Owen refers to himself as 'Art' throughout his papers, so we will do the same. The new family lived at 22 Lower Bennett Street in Greenwich; the area was rebuilt in the last century, but the house was less than a mile from the River Thames. Arthur Robert was 25; he had had a range of jobs associated with shipping on the River Thames since he was 14. In 1877 he was working as the master of the sea going paddle tug, the 'Dreadnought', towing sailing ships in and out of the Thames into the English Channel. In his memoirs he mentioned working with the Cutty Sark, which today is preserved at Greenwich.

Steam tugs would go out of London, around Kent into the English Channel and literally wait for the next big sailing ship that came along; and then try and do a deal over the cost of towing the bigger ship into London. Using a steam tug made absolute sense in the River Thames; and a lot of sense in the area around Kent. If you have a fair wind to come up the Channel, then it may not be from the right direction to enable you to sail northwards and then westwards to the entrance to the River Thames. Entertaining job, being the Master of a tug; you were the first person from the outside world that people on the sailing ship would have seen for some time. 'What's happened in the last three months?'

The River Thames seems to have been in Arthur Robert's blood, somehow; he said later that his earliest memory was being taken by his nurse to see the launching of Brunel's ship, the 'Great Eastern' in 1858, when he would have been six!

London was the largest city in the world, the capital of the British Empire, and the world's largest port. Increased trade and growth in the size of ships meant that new docks were being built; in 1880 the Royal Albert Dock was opened, and the results of the continued investment were obvious. In that year the Port of London received 8 million tons of goods, a 10-fold increase on the 800,000 received in 1800.

But work associated with River was unstable, varying with the season and the vagaries of world trade. It was also, in part at least, a closed shop: Arthur Robert was licensed as a Freeman to the 'Company of Watermen and Lightermen of the River Thames' (which traces its history as a Guild back to 1555) and that was probably the key to getting work.

The family grew. Art was soon joined by his brothers Ernest, born in 1879, Walter in 1880 and Leonard in 1882. Arthur Robert must have planned early on for his sons to have stable, well paid jobs. For at least three of his sons, he fastened on the idea of them becoming Thames Pilots.

We tend to think, these days, of a pilot as being someone in charge of an aeroplane, but in the maritime sense, a Pilot is the 'local expert' for a given port; they went on board the ship as it left dock and took responsibility for

Four brothers, taken about 1900.

From left, Leonard, (a future Thames Pilot), Walter, Art and Ernest.

guiding the ship down the river and into the sea. They knew where sandbanks and wrecks were, and the right channel for a ship of a given size. The shipping channel is not always in the middle of the river! Once the ship was safely out into the sea, the Pilot was picked up by a smaller boat and ferried back to shore.

The first step for Art was in July 1888, when, at the age of 11, he went to the Royal Hospital School. Though now based in Suffolk, it was until 1933 in Greenwich, in buildings now occupied by the University of Greenwich. It has always had a tradition of preparing boys for service in either the Royal or Merchant navies. From Art's point of view the good news was that the school was literally less than a mile from the family home.

Among other training aids was a full size fully rigged mast. Imagine climbing to the top of that as an eleven year old!

He must have shown some aptitude for life in the school, because we have a certificate confirming that he was a chief petty officer in possession of three good conduct badges. It further says that because his conduct and seamanship were 'very good' he could count his time in the school as worth a year off qualifying for competency in the Mercantile Marine. In July 1892, the year before he left, the school held a prizegiving ceremony where Art picked up three prizes.

Prize giving certificate from the Greenwich Royal Hospital School. July 1892

It seems as if Art's father was a persuasive guy; or maybe what we think of as a Victorian Father. Arthur Newton, as a teenager, said 'Yes, Pa' and went along with the idea of training to become a Thames Pilot. So at the age of 16, he was apprenticed to a Captain Coles, the Master of the sailing ship Mermerus' for a period of three years. His father had to pay £30 for Art to become an apprentice; maybe two months wages for a professional. It's equally possible that Art was a stroppy teenager; how many parents today would welcome the idea of their dear teenage son being sent to Australia?!

The Mermerus was in the Australian wool trade, which grew from the 1860's through to the turn of the century, as Australia was settled, and agriculture became the main occupation of emigrants.

This was a pretty prestigious ship to be in. Mermerus was probably amongst the biggest of the sailing ships around at the time she was built; 80 m long, and nearly 50 m from the deck to the top of the main mast. That's equivalent to a 20 storey building; climbed without any safety netting!
The ships of the wool fleet made the journey from Melbourne to London in anything from 70 to 110 days, and made one round trip each year. They left London in April or May, loaded wool in October and early November (the start of the Australian summer) and aimed to arrive in London for the sales in February.

Sail plan of Mermerus

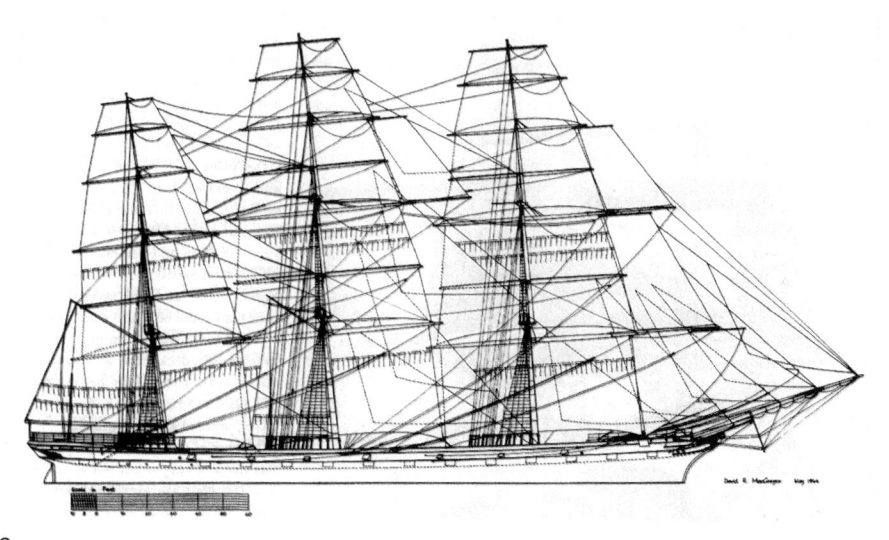

She was one of the ships in the 'Golden Fleece' line, owned by A & JH Carmichael & Co, based in Greenock in Scotland. She was built in 1872, so by the time Art joined her, she was certainly no longer a new ship. She was, however, still fast; in 1896, she sailed from Melbourne to London in 76 days; quite respectable!

> Saturday 1st April 1893. Joined "Mermerus" 8 A.M. Left East India Dock at 1 P.M. Pa and Ma came to Gravesend. Bid them goodbye. Wind fresh. Dead east. Wrote home 8 o'clock by pilot. Put in starboard watch. Watch 6-8, 12-4. Full moon. A lovely night. Turned in at 9:30.

By Tuesday, they were in the Bay of Biscay, some 500 miles from London.

> Tuesday 4th. Wind Easterly. Sea very rough, but weather fine. Was sick in the morning and felt queer all day. Wished I was at home. Ate nothing all day. In the Bay of Biscay. Oh!

> Wednesday 5th. Washed decks 5:30 A.M. Felt a little better, rather homesick. Nothing much occurred. Went aloft for first time to main top. Weather fine. Cleared my box out.

Having been to the Royal Hospital School didn't prepare Art completely for life at sea; probably nothing would!

> Tuesday 11th April 1893. Calm continued all day. Washed decks 5:30 A.M. Morning in; had a read. Weather awfully hot. Reached Latitude. 28 1/2° N. Slight breeze towards evening. Squared yards. Rate about 2 miles. Left off pants. Prepared for tropics. Turned in at 8:30 P.M. I found that work was very hard at this time and wished I had not gone, but I suppose I shall get used to it. It is too late to give up now. Wish I had known what it was like before I came, though.

The latitude that he quotes places them to the west of the Canary Islands.

In 1894, Art's second year in the Mermerus, things were less straightforward. They left London on the 7th June; the ship being towed by a steam powered tug, as on the first voyage, until 3.00pm on the next day, when they were off Beachy Head. The wind was generally from the west.

Which of course is the wrong direction if you are trying to sail westwards down the English Channel! Could sailing ships sail into the wind? Yes and no; not directly into the wind, but well handled, they could sail at an angle of up to 45 degrees off the direction of the wind. So if the wind was blowing from the west, she could sail North west or South west, but not in between. If they then got too close to land, the ship has to be turned; either by 'tacking' or 'wearing' the ship.

> Saturday 9th June, 1894. Wind still westerly, light. Sent up main royal yard and sail. Tacked ship at varied intervals, particularly in our watches below. Fine evening, getting damp towards night. Somewhat between Beachy Head and Isle of Wight. Plenty of craft of all descriptions about.

The ship was now zig-zagging across the English Channel. They were off the Isle of Wight by 11pm on the 10th June, and then off the French coast at 6am on the morning of the 11th.

> Monday 11th. Wind still westerly strong. Ushant bore South South East about 7 miles at 8 in the evening.

Ushant is the island off the westernmost point of Brittany, 110 miles to the south east of the Scilly Islands. So they had taken 4 days to sail the length of the English Channel. Overall the 1894 voyage to Australia took 91 days, arriving in Melbourne on the 6th September.

I mentioned an apprenticeship for Art; this was 1893; why take an apprenticeship on a sailing ship, even one as prestigious as a wool clipper? Surely steam ships were the up and coming thing?

But In 1890, just less than half of the cargo coming into London was still carried in sailing ships. They were a well established, mostly reliable, way of transporting goods around the world.

Part of the answer to the question of 'Why sailing ships?' seems to be that the skills learnt in a sailing ship remained in demand. For years the best 'graduates' were recruited by the big steamship lines; Cunard, White Star, P and O and so on. These companies required all their watch keeping officers to be qualified in sail; to have a solid basis of sound seamanship, and the calm ability to handle emergencies.

The modern simile is probably in taking a driving test. If you are qualified only to drive an automatic car, you are going to be stuck if suddenly you need to cope with gear changes. A Thames Pilot only qualified to deal with a steamship would not be able to deal with the problems generated by a large sailing ship!

Alan Villiers describes the system of apprenticeship:

> '....boys of 14 and upwards to 16/17 could be bound to an owner to work for him for four years in his ships for nothing (sometimes a pittance in the fourth year). The usual premium charged was £40 for each lad, which was a lot of money in 1895 or 1915. For this sum paid by their parents, four, six or eight hardy lads slept in a steel 'house' in the wettest part of the ship, where they had rough bunks, their own sea chests to sit on and their strict allowance of food like the foremast hands. Some ships were worse than others, but often the boys had not enough to eat at sea or in port. Instruction was minimal.'

The system of apprenticeship was good news for the ship owners; in the wool trade, some years before, the Cutty Sark had 8 able seamen and 8 apprentices, plus specialists like the sailmaker and the carpenter. Being paid, rather than paying, for nearly half the crew sounds good value for money for the owner of the ship!

On his first voyage home from Australia, Art noted in his diary

Four apprentices on board the 'Mermerus' 1895.

that the Mermerus had five apprentices on board; two of them, Art and Jerry were still on board the ship in 1895, and a photo of them has survived. Art, by then, looks very much the experienced seaman!

It was, however, a heck of a way to learn a trade; here are his log entries for two days towards the end of his second voyage from London to Melbourne. They are in the middle of the Southern Ocean; the nearest decent bit of land is Antarctica!

> Friday 17th August 1894. Wind freshened at 3:30 A.M. giving 13 knots. Handed crojack and main topgallants. All hands called at 6 A.M. Reduced to 3 lower topsails. Gale still blowing heavily from the WNW with heavy rain. Set reefed topsail at 4 P.M. Still bitterly cold. Continually filling herself. This weather is something fearful. Shall be jolly glad to get in. Latitude 43° 40' S, Longitude. 71° 7' E. 229 miles sailed today.
>
> Saturday 18th. Gale increasing, until by the afternoon it was blowing with hurricane force. Made mizzen. topsail fast at noon and main upper topsail at 3 P.M. The sea something indescribable. At 6:30 P.M. in a tremendous squall, wind suddenly shifted to the South South west. All hands called immediately, to brace up the yards. Ship full up. Hands can hardly pull on braces; only their heads visible, the seas meanwhile washing from side to side with tremendous force. Rolling terribly, very nearly broaching to. Almost aback; another point and the sticks (masts) would have gone, and the ship would have swamped and gone down in a minute. Captain remarked to the Mate that it was a "case of touch and go." Immediately afterwards, the wind fell light on starboard quarter, and continued so throughout the night. It has been blowing a strong gale all the week. Scarcely a stroke done, hands standing by. Latitude. 44° 3' S, Longitude. 76° 5' E. 249 miles sailed
>
> Just over two weeks later, they were tied up in the calm of the harbour at Melbourne!

2   Seamanship

Art's diary entries are sometimes almost written in shorthand; the terminology that he uses is really only completely comprehensible to someone used to square rigged ships. I wonder who he thought he was writing them for? Himself alone, or his father? (who would have probably understood what he was on about, though he spent most of his working life in steam powered ships). I can't imagine that he thought that his grandsons would be reading his diaries 120 years later. On his first voyage, we can see that he is gradually trusted with more complicated tasks; he is learning the ropes!

> Saturday 20th May 1893. Turned out 7:30 A.M. Weather same. Breeze the same. High sea running. Kept poop all the morning. Sun shone a bit. Saw a whale. Turned in, in afternoon. Long night out. Very squally. Found it was a bit different keeping night watches with oilskins, stockings, sea boots, etc., on in dirty weather to what it was wearing them at home. Captain Coles sent me aloft to furl mizen topgallants, staysail. First heavy job aloft. Long. 6° E.

I imagine that even in the years at the end of the 19th century, with steam engines powering more and more and more ships, those people in the sailing ship business would have assumed that ships would have gone on being powered by the wind. The idea that within 50 years there simply wouldn't be any commercial sailing ships would have seemed astonishing to them: why would you give up a source of free power!

Alan Villiers makes the point that the way sailing ships operated had evolved over the centuries, and that, by and large, all square rigged ships worked in the same way. A sailor from Drake's 'Golden Hind' of 1580 would soon understand how everything worked in Nelson's 'Victory' of 1800, and would be a useful hand aboard in his first sea watch; a sailor from the 'Victory', though appalled at the size of everything and the smallness of the crew, would rapidly know his way around a ship like the Mermerus.

Ropes were secured in the same place, each time they were used; they had to be, otherwise when sail had to be taken in in the middle of the night (no torches!) the seamen might undo the wrong rope; chaos!

There is a nice story by Rudyard Kipling called 'Captains Courageous' about a spoilt brat of a teenager who falls overboard from a passenger liner and is picked up by a fishing schooner on the Grand Banks, off Newfoundland. As part of his 'education' he is walked around the schooner until he knows the purpose of every rope. Without that knowledge he is a danger to everyone else on board. Literally, he was 'Learning the ropes'.

Villiers, writing in the 1950's mourns the loss of that knowledge; even walking around the 'Cutty Sark' in Greenwich will only, at best, give you half the information; because she demonstrates what is called the 'standing rigging' which held the masts up, and which could be adjusted but, by and large didn't get moved. The 'running rigging' which controlled the sails is there, but isn't operable because, of course, hoisting sails on a ship bolted to the ground would lead quickly to something breaking!

So what ropes did Art have to learn on his first voyage? I'm not an expert by any stretch of the imagination; find a copy of Alan Villiers 'The Way of a Ship', but it seems to me that there were three key groups of ropes. The first were the braces. The square sails were fixed to the yards, which in turn were fixed to the masts. The yards could be turned in a horizontal movement, so that the maximum amount of sail could be exposed to the wind, and the ropes that did that were the braces; attached to the ends of the yards, and then eventually brought down to the deck. As the ropes attached to one end of the yard was pulled in, so, by definition, the ropes at the other end had to be let out. All the yards on a given mast would be moved together; in larger ships built at the end of the 19th century all the braces for a mast would be brought to a 'brace winch' which controlled the movement of all of the yards in one go; much safer for everybody concerned.

Friday 22nd December. Hardly any wind. Course ENE. Weather unbearably hot. Very clear. Started painting over side (the ports). Nearly finished by evening. A grand sunset. Dead calm. A sea like glass. Full moon. A most glorious night. The best we have had since leaving home. Bos'uns' gang set up mizen rigging, also mizen topgallant and royal stays. Dead silence almost - not a sound to be heard but an occasional flutter of the sails against the mast and the half-hour chiming of the bell. Second mate took a fit about 10:30 P.M. and braced all the yard round on the other tack. Thought he felt wind, I suppose, but the ship lay like a log all night.

The second group of ropes were those that controlled the setting of the sail. Attached to the bottom corner of each of the square sails were the sheets. They ran from the corner of the sails to the end of the yard below; pulled tight they stretched the sail out and secured it in place; again, they were brought down to deck level to be operated and secured. Anyone who has sailed on a small boat will recognise that the same name, and rope is still in use.

When a sail had to be taken in, of course, the sheets would be let out; but the sail would be full of wind, and would quickly get out of control. The popular image is of men standing in the rigging fighting to control the sail, but there were ways of reducing the amount of work they had to do. 'Bunt lines' were fastened to the bottom edge of the sail, ran at intervals up its front face up to the yard (and then down to the deck); a close relative, the 'leech line' was fastened to the side edge of the sail. When the sail needed to be furled, the bunt and leech lines would be pulled in at the same time as the sheet was released, and the combination of the three meant that as much as possible of the sail was hauled up tight to the yard above. Only then would the crew venture out onto the yard to pull in the last of the slack canvas and secure it with short ropes called gaskets.

From Art's diary it's clear that sails were taken in in a particular order as the wind strength increased. The royals at the top of the mast would be taken in first, then the topgallants, divided, in the Mermerus, into two to reduce the amount of canvas involved. The next sails down, the topsails (again split into upper and lower topsails) were actually the last to be taken in; before them the courses, the biggest sails at the bottom of the pyramid would be furled. As wind strength eased, the process was reversed. Fine judgement was called for from the Captain and the Mates as to how much sail a ship could carry in a given wind strength and sea condition. Too much and something would break; too little and the ship wouldn't be going as fast as she could do.

Not being able to use either the Panama or Suez canals, ships like the Mermerus travelled out to Australia via the South Atlantic, passing to the south of the Cape of Good Hope, and then returned through the Southern Ocean, passing Cape Horn. In those southern latitudes, the weather and associated sea conditions could be dreadful. In November 1893 on his first voyage on the Mermerus, they were on their way home; in the Southern Ocean, between Australia and South America.

> Sunday 26th November 1893. Heavy sea still running. Shipping seas every minute. Course North east by East. Wind from the West South West. Heavy squalls of sleet, etc. Bitterly cold. On poop all the time. In longitude. 139°, latitude about 51° S. Hands can hardly walk aft because of the seas breaking on deck. In house, washing about inside with gear etc. Everything wet. The worst Sunday we have had. Icebergs plentiful, of all sizes. Fore topsail chafed through. Sail maker aloft from 7 til 11:30 P.M. mending it. Frequent squalls of rain, hail, and sleet.

Mermerus in Melbourne

Monday 27th. Wind still blowing awfully strong, with very heavy sea. Shortened down to single main topsail. Going 11 knots all day. Still bitterly cold. Course East by North 1/2 North. Wind slacked a little towards 7 P.M. Set 4 topsails and foresail. Going 11 knots during night. Shortened down again.

Each voyage that Art made seems to contain at least one account of a 'near disaster'. On the same voyage, they had rounded Cape Horn, and were in the South Atlantic, roughly to the east of the Falkland Islands.

Wednesday 13th December 1893. Cleared up towards morning. Set all sail again. Going 10 knots North East by North 1/2 North. Scrubbed bulwarks in afternoon. Night moderately clear to about 12:30 P.M. Suddenly found ourselves almost on tremendous iceberg. Lookout never saw it. An awful moment. Helm put hard up just in time. Cleared it by about 12 feet. Watch below called immediately. Took in all light sails. One minute later and we should have met a fearful fate. Sighted several more icebergs during the night. Another man and officer put on the lookout. All the brightwork covered with canvas. Latitude. 46° 49' S, Longitude. 45° 37' W.

By the January 1894, homeward bound on Art's first voyage, the Mermerus has sailed a good way northwards. He has spent 9 months on the ship, and is clearly trusted to work with the other seamen on changing the sails from the lighter weight ones to heavy weather ones. 'Winter North Atlantic' is the most serious category of weather; the sails need to suit the conditions that the ship is likely to meet.

Monday 15th January 1894. Wind inclined to drop. Rather unsteady. A heavy swell from the WNW. Sent down the foresail, mainsail, and fore and main lower topsails, sending up the heavy weather ones in their places. Enormous quantities of gulf weed off the bow. Lat. 25° 20 N, Long. 38° 49' W. N 3/4 W. 220 miles.

Tuesday 16th January. Wind still very unsteady. Weather mild and clear. Bent the fore and main upper topsails and topgallant sails, also mizzen upper topsail and fore and main topmast staysails. Night clear. Heavy dew. Lat. 28° 30 N, Long. 37° 17' W. 190 miles.

By the last day of January, they are about 250 miles to the south west of England, but the weather is dreadful.

> <u>Wednesday 31st</u>. Blew a gale of wind all last night with very heavy squalls and a tremendous sea running. Enormous swell from the NW. Wind from same quarter. Course E by N 1/2 N. A barque sighted on port bow at dawn, homeward bound. Right astern at 5 P.M. An awful night - bitterly cold. Hauled up foresail, lowered upper topsails and fore topmast staysail. Made all fast. Going 7 knots all night under lower topsails and trysail. Weather awfully cold, with frequent falls of hail and sleet. Blew especially hard in middle watch. Got below at 9:30 P.M. Lat. 47° 17 N, Long. 11° 47' W.

For almost all of the voyage home from Australia, Art notes the position of the ship at the end of almost every entry. I assume that he must have copied these from the official log of the ship kept by the Master; but maybe part of his training required him to make the calculations himself, based on the use of his sextant and reference to the ship's chronometer.

We had his sextant; my Dad presented it to the National Museum of Wales, thinking that they would put it on display. They said 'Thank you very much' and put it in their store; I hope it's still there somewhere!

Moshulu, South Atlantic. Newby

It must have been interesting, though; January and February in the North Atlantic are not noted for clear skies. If your position depends on taking a sight of stars or sun with a sextant, inaccuracies must have crept in. How are they going to know where they are when it comes to sailing up the Channel?

On one of his voyages they 'cast the lead'; using a long line with a weight on the bottom to establish the depth of the water. If it was shallow(ish) you were getting close. One not infallible clue was the number of other ships they saw; another, slightly surprisingly, was the colour of the water.

> Thursday 1st February 1894 Morning broke with sea a bit quieter; wind not quite as strong and squalls less frequent, more occurring after 5 A.M. Set reefed fore topsail and whole mizen topsail in morning watch. Going at about 7 knots all day, till evening, when a good steady 9-10 knot set in. Shook reefs out of main topsail and set main topgallants and crojack. Course ENE. Water changing colour rapidly. About 130 miles off Lizards at noon. Passed a steamer (German) and barquentine very closely during afternoon. Sighted two steamers masthead lights in 2nd dog watch. Both appearing on starboard bow and vanishing on beam. Outside the Channel. Lat. 48° 44 N, Long. 7° 45' W.

Finally, infallibly, they sight land. A corporate sigh of relief!

> Friday 2nd. Water very light in colour. Got into the Channel with a good 10 knot breeze right aft. Start Point sighted at 9:15 A.M., on the beam 10:15 A.M. Plenty of vessels of all descriptions about. Portland Bill passed 3 P.M. St. Alban's Head on beam at 5 P.M. St. Catherine's Point 7:30 P.M. Owers Light vessel at 9 P.M. Looked threatening astern. Commenced breezing up. Handed foresail 6 P.M. Reefed main and fore topsails and made them and mizzen topsail fast. Lights of all colours around us. Beachy Head in sight.

> Saturday 3rd. Blew very strong at 2 A.M. Hove to till morning. Heading S. Rather foggy with heavy rain. Squared in at 9 A.M. Wind a little on port quarter. Passed Beachy Head. Took tug and pilot off Dungeness. Passed Dover at 5 P.M. Made all sails fast.

Sunday 4th. Anchored off the Nore 4:15 A.M. Weighed anchor at 5 A.M. and proceeded up the river, passing Gravesend at 9 A.M. and Greenwich 11:30. Went into the London Docks. I left at 3:30 P.M. and arrived home safely at 4:30 P.M. after a 10 months' trip.

"MERMERUS" alongside.

I was on board when this photograph was taken, November, 1894. Dad.

Mermerus in Melbourne; 1894 from Lubbock.
Annotated by Art.

3   Conditions

Mermerus was, for those times, a big ship. The wool clippers docked in London in the East India Docks, to the east of what is now the Canary Wharf development. They sailed from there in the April of each year, arriving in Australia in June or July in the middle of the Australian winter. They loaded with wool in October, as the Australian summer approached, and sheep were sheared, and arrived back in London in January or February. It seems strange now that they did one voyage per year, but the logic, of course, is that sheep are sheared once a year.

The aim of every skipper was to arrive just in time for a sale, because an extra cost was involved if the bales of wool had to be held in warehouses. Art's ship, the Mermerus, seemed to leave Melbourne with a view to arriving in London in time for the February wool sale, and had a reputation for reliability.

The Mermerus carried 10,000 bales of wool, which represented the fleeces of 1,000,000 sheep. The value of the entire cargo of the Mermerus could be £130,000 in 1895. In modern money that would be in the region of £8 million.

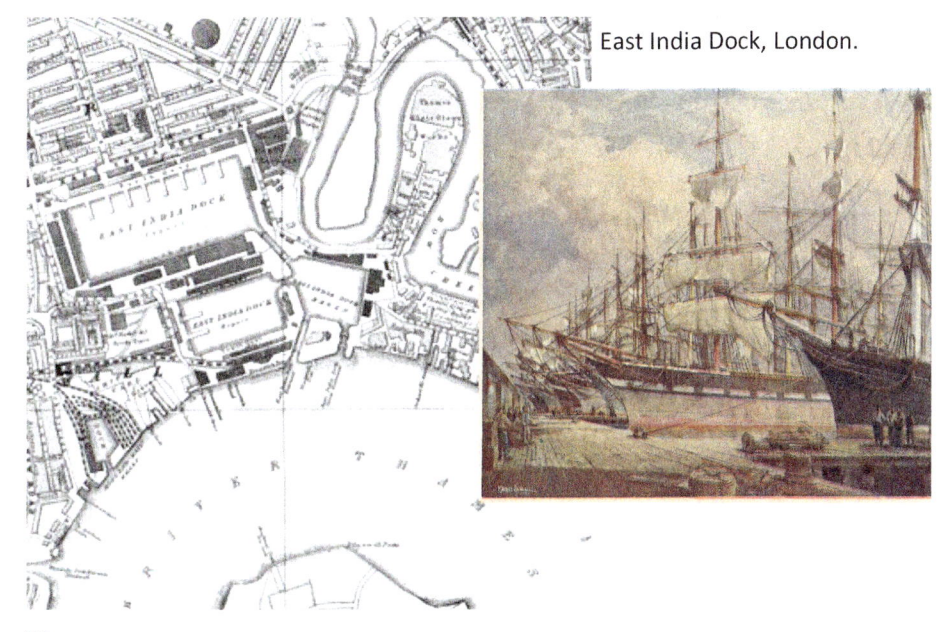

East India Dock, London.

The value of the wool was massively more than the cost of building the ship. It's a bit like the modern situation where the value of the goods on a supermarket's shelves is often more than the cost of creating the building. In effect the ship was a floating warehouse that also brought the wool from Australia to the UK. That didn't mean to say that there was a vast amount of profit to be made by the ship owner; it was important to keep the costs of running the ship as low as possible, because the new versions of steam ships were becoming cheaper to run.

The aim was to squeeze as much wool as possible into the ship. In his diary, Art doesn't talk about the loading operation much; presumably that was the responsibility of stevedores, but the Captain of the ship would both want to squeeze in the maximum amount of cargo, and have it done in such a way as to give the ship the correct trim; the way she floated in the water.

I suppose that could dramatically affect her overall speed and the way she behaved on the water. Get it wrong and the ship would be uncontrollable. It sounds as if wool ought to be an easy cargo to deal with, but apparently if it was packed when it was wet, it could spontaneously burst into flame. You really don't want that to happen at sea. My Dad had a little plaque in his workshop which said 'An accident at sea could ruin your whole day'!

Basil Greenhill, the former Director of the Maritime Museum at Greenwich, summarises the reasons why sail gave way to steam. By 1865 the transport of tea from China to the UK, for which ships like the Cutty Sark were built, was as good as lost to sailing ships. Some of them, like the Cutty Sark, were moved to the Australian trade, taking coal, manufactured goods and emigrants out, and bringing grain and wool back to Britain. In the 1870's, when Mermerus was built, something of a balance existed between the running costs of the compound-engined steam ship and sail. But then, in the 1880's the triple expansion steam engine was perfected, and steel became readily available for boilers.

A writer called Robin Craig has come up with a vivid illustration. A first class cargo steamer of the late years of Queen Victoria's reign could carry one ton of cargo one mile using the heat in her furnace generated by burning one sheet of high quality Victorian writing paper.

By the middle of the 1890's, when Art was an apprentice, the sailing ships must have been struggling to compete with steamships; in fact in 1898, the year after Art finished his apprenticeship, the Mermerus was sold to new owners based in Finland; she was probably no longer making any money in the wool trade.

To remain competitive, the owners must have tried to keep all running costs to a minimum, including that of keeping the crew alive. Art listed the food that they got on the sixth day of his first voyage; clearly high on the priority list for a hungry 16 year old!

> <u>Thursday 6th April 1893</u>. Felt much better. My morning watch. Sighted another sailing ship. Signalled to her. Capt. Coles gave me charge of flags. Weather warm. Wind North east, changing to East towards evening. Sea rough. Saw phosphorine in water for first time. Bread on Sunday, Tuesday and Thursday.
>
> Pea soup every other day.
>
> Salt junk on pork every day.
>
> Sugar every Saturday.
>
> Coffee for breakfast and tea for tea. Also coffee at 5 A.M. on wash-down mornings.
>
> Marmalade every week.

It doesn't sound as if they were over-fed, and there certainly wasn't much variety. The pork was rubbed with salt to preserve it; refrigeration wasn't readily available until the middle of the twentieth century. But it must have made you so thirsty; and there certainly weren't unlimited supplies of fresh water. And imagine eating it every day!

These are hungry young men; my grandsons, now of much the same age as Art at this time, just absorb food, and he is working very hard.

There can't have been much difference between this diet and that enjoyed, if that's the right word, by the men who went to sea with Nelson!

In early 1894 on his first voyage home, Art listed the supplies he needed to have for his next voyage; food features close to the top of the list!

Things which the other fellows brought.

> Methylated spirit stove and kettle. Jams, pickles, cake, puddings, cocoa, butter, sardines, tinned meats and fruits, table jellies, milk, biscuits.
>
> Also pictures, bunk curtains, photo frames.

Want for next voyage:

A palm and needles.

Some cotton ties.

Cloth trousers (ordinary).

1 thick, warm knockabout.

Alan Villiers (who was one of the last people with the experience and qualifications to a captain of a big sailing ship) makes the point that the sailing ship, even a big one such as the Mermerus, built of steel and well maintained, was also dangerous. Sailing without an engine or radio, even in the early 20th century it was not unusual in some years for 10 or 12 big square riggers to go missing.

This is from Art's second voyage in the Mermerus, in 1894. They are in the Southern Ocean.

> <u>Thursday 16th August 1894.</u> A sad thing occurred this morning at 3 A.M. The wind suddenly freshening, mate gave the order, "Main topgallant downhauls." Two seamen, Lowe and Duncan with Jerrard went to lee one, when a tremendous sea came over to leeward, carrying poor Lowe over and washing Duncan and Jerrard forward. Jerrard getting severely bruised. This only the second man Captain Coles has lost. Filled herself with water several times. Course South East by East 1/2 East. 10 knots. Set crojack and fore and mizen upper topsail. Latitude. 43° 37' S, Long. 66° 01' E. 280 miles.

So it's the middle of the night; the wind is getting stronger, so there is a need to take in the topgallant sails on the main mast. Three men go to haul on the appropriate ropes, which are all secured at deck level; a wave comes in over the side of the ship, and washes all three of them forward. Two of them, Jerrard (who is another of the apprentices) and Duncan wash up against something, but Coles disappears clean overboard. There was nothing that could be done; no-one wore lifejackets, which would have simply got in the way most of the time; it's the middle of the night, and the ship is moving at 10 knots. They are in the middle of the Southern Ocean, with Antarctica the nearest land, about 1300 miles to the south. The water would have been very cold.

It must have affected the entire crew. Art comments in his diary the next day; 'I shall be jolly glad to get in'.

A final example; this time from Art's third voyage in the Mermerus; in the Southern Ocean again, but this time further to the east; roughly half way between South Africa and their destination in South Australia, Melbourne.

> Friday 19th July 1895. 3:30 A.M. all hands set trysail and furled mizzen topsail. Wind increased to a gale by this time. "All hands" called again at 7:15 A.M. to furl fore topsails. Down to the old original canvas once more. Rolling something fearfully; full up with water all day long. The sea at noon was something frightful, being the worst I have ever seen. The captain observed afterwards that from 12-2 P.M. was the worst four hours he had ever had at sea. He was expecting to see his masts go every minute. Rolling to over 45°. Four oil bags out. Mizzen royal blew right out of its gaskets. Gale abated a bit in dog watches. Set fore lower topsail and fore topmast staysail and scudded before it again. Latitude. 43° 48' South, Longitude. 83° 22' East.

The Mermerus is sailing under the absolute minimum number of sails; maybe just one sail, or perhaps one on each mast. She is rolling from side to side, through an overall angle of 90 degrees. That means that at each side of that roll the rail on the edge of the deck must have been underwater; so, yes, the deck is full of water all the time. The strain on the standing rigging which held the masts up must have been enormous; if one rope went the mast would have probably gone, and since the whole system of masts and rigging was interlinked, that would leave the ship unstable, and without any means of propulsion: Not good!

Saturday 4th August 1895. Wind moderated a little with daybreak. Set all sail again. Fine day, but cold. Going 10 knots South East 1/2 East. Making sennit, foxes, etc. Wind increased towards midnight; commenced shortening sail in 1st watch, until by 4 o'clock (Sunday A.M.) we were once more under 4 topsails and foresail. Blowing a strong gale. Tremendous squalls all night, snow, sleet, hail, etc. and vivid lightning. Fearful sea on. Shipping immense quantities of water. Bitterly cold. Wished I was on the

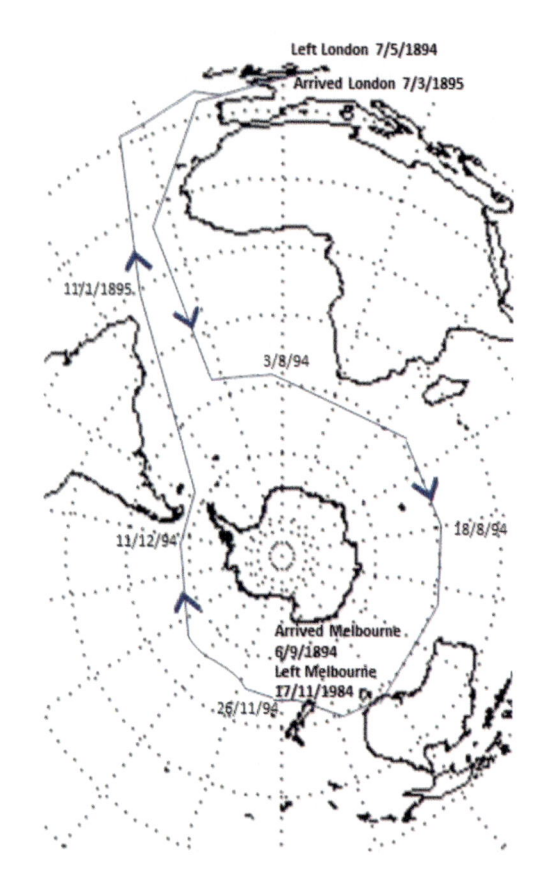

Mermerus' 1894-95 voyage

"Kohinoor." Latitude. 40° 21' S, Longitude. 3° 15' E. 211 miles sailed in the day.

By now Arthur Robert, Art's father was the Master of the 'Kohinoor', a paddle steamer owned by the Victoria Steamboat Co. She took passengers on pleasure trips from the centre of London (she could lower her two funnels to enable her to just fit through the arches of London Bridge) to places like Margate, on the north Kent coast. For Art life was less peaceful in the South Atlantic!

I've read somewhere that war consists of long periods of boredom punctuated by moments of sheer terror; I think Art's time at sea was like that!

4 Setting the sails

The aim in a big sailing ship must have been to change the setting of the sails as little as possible. They used more sails in light winds, and took them in when the winds grew stronger. They adjusted the setting of them depending on where the wind was blowing from, relative to the course the ship wanted to follow.

They were helped that winds in the big oceans blow in consistent directions; they are known as Trade Winds. Once the ship got into those life was a bit simpler, but in between, in the Atlantic, is the area around the Equator known as the doldrums, with no consistent wind at all.

In his 1895 voyage he records leaving the NE trades as they approach the equator:

> Friday 31st May 1895. Watch fearfully hot, with scarcely any wind. Lost the NE Trades. Finished off fore lanyards (throat seizings, etc.) Rounding on main crane lines, and canvas on sheer poles. Box-hauled yards a bit. Sky very heavy and dull. Doldrums commencing. Tremendous fall of rain in first watch. Lat. 7° 32' N, Long. 24° 23' W.

By the daytime of the 2nd June there is still no consistent wind; but notice the figure he gives for the latitude; the number is going down as they approach the equator; that's Latitude 0 degrees.

> Sunday 2nd June 1895. Very dull, stormy-looking day. Heavy banks of clouds all round, and not a breath of air to keep you cool. Fearfully oppressive. Sleep in bunks impossible. Squalls flying around at intervals. Courses hauled up, skysail and mizzen royal fast. This is "doldrums" with a vengeance. Whit Sunday today. S.E. Trades set in during first watch. Beautiful night. Lat. 5° 25' N, Long. 23° 16' W.

But the S E trades have started to blow.

> Monday 3rd. Bank holiday (not here, though). Beautiful weather; terribly hot, but with grand breeze from SSE. Course SW by W, about 8 knots. Overhauled davits and gear, also lifeboats, and fitted them. Overhauled blocks of gear of courses, also port fore brace

Doldrums, thunder about.

Watercolour painting by AJA Owen: Art's son and my father!

brace blocks. Put off ends of fore lanyards equally, and finished them off. Yards sharp up to port. Night very fine. Lat. 3° 27' N, Long. 23° 32' W.

By the next day the wind is blowing from the South South east; the ship can use that (with, as he says the yards braced sharp up to port), and can manage a course of South west by west. There is the word 'south' at the start of that direction; that's good enough!

It's interesting that he doesn't use degrees to measure the direction of the wind; he uses the points of the compass. We are all used to North, East, South and West, but Art is dividing it up a lot further; first of all into NE, SE, SW and NW, and then each of those further. In total into sections of 11 1/4 degrees; good enough to describe the course of a ship, or the direction of the wind.

So what did the crew do, when the sails didn't need adjusting? They maintained the ship.

Almost every day in Art's diary has a reference to scraping something or painting something, or maintaining the rigging. Here's a sample, eight days later than the last entry above.

> Tuesday 11<u>th</u> June 1895. Weather still very fine; wind very fresh. Averaging 9 knots, SW, until noon. "About ship" at 8 bells. Making E by N 1/2 N on other tack. First time we have had to tack this voyage. Moderate sea. Overhauled fore, and all topsail footropes, and main topgallant, lift lanyard. Repaired fore and main sheets. Rove new fore upper topgallant braces, and crojack bowline. Repaired mizzen topgallant, keel lines, and put gilguys on mizzen. topmast backstays, and mizzen topgallant rigging. Very squally all night. Handed fore and main royals in middle watch. Lat. 15° 12' S, Long. 37° 48' W.

The footropes are the ropes under each yard that the sailors could stand on. The 'blocks' are pulleys through which the ropes passed: made of wood with metal wheels inside them, they needed to be checked regularly. If the rope passing through one of them jammed, then chaos would ensue!

The rigging of a ship like the Mermerus contained miles of rope, of various sizes; each one responsible for doing something, and important in its own way. All of the rope could fray; particularly where it passed through a block. All of it had to be checked and replaced if necessary, regularly.

The masts were the same. The lower masts and lower yards were made of steel (the main yard, carrying the largest sail, was a whopping 88 feet (27 m) long; using the traditional unit of British measurement, four cricket pitches!

But the upper masts and yards would have been made of pitch pine; which needed to be checked for splits and varnished or painted regularly.

All of the work in the rigging would have been done from the yards which held the sails (where there was a footrope to stand on underneath the yard; but you would need to hold on with one hand while you worked with the other; difficult) or what was called a 'bosun's chair; basically a swing seat suspended in the rigging from some fixed point above.

Neither easy; dropping a paintbrush was probably a hanging offence. Where do you get a new one in the middle of the ocean?!

In terms of overall health, I suppose the crew of the ship were isolated for three months at a time, so every-day bugs would have worked their way out of the system. There were always going to be problems associated with heavy labour. In his 1895 voyage, his third and final one on the Mermerus, they were on their way home from Australia.

> Monday 16<u>th</u> September 1895. Making 9 knots all day, with fine steady breeze just a little on port quarter. All sails set. Overhauled and oiled fore and main topgallant braces. Reputtied bad seams on poop deck. Painted anchors. Also continued making sennit. On turning out this morning, found a large swelling on my left knee, making walking very painful. Kept my afternoon watch on deck as usual, but captain sent me below at 6 P.M. Put a huge poultice on. Lat. 51° 49 S, Long. 175° 16' W. 224 miles.

The next day Art describes the pain as being 'something awful'. The day after that, he was confined to his bunk.

> Wednesday 18th. Gale moderating a bit, but tremendous sea on. Put topsails on her in forenoon; had all sails, excepting mainsail and royals and light staysails, on her in first dog watch. Shipping a little water, rolling very heavily at times. Hands standing by in morning; working at odd jobs in afternoon. Not the least difference in my knee; the pain being cruel at times, so I cannot bear the weight of a poultice on it. Passed a restless night. Captain painted it with iodine. Gave me beans. Lat. 50° 40' S, Long. 162° 56' W. 250 miles.

I wonder what the beans were supposed to do?! Two days later it was no better.

> Friday 20th. Captain came for'ard this morning, and told me that he was having a bunk fixed up for me aft. Two or three hands carried me there at 7 A.M. The old man could not be behaving more kindly to me were I his own son; he does not seem to be able to do enough for me.

Gives me every possible thing I could want, journals to read without number. I have only to ring a bell, and the steward is in attendance upon me at once. Mr. Dayoete (our gentleman passenger) also very kind. He acts as assistant surgeon when the poulticing operations are underway. Leg very painful all the forenoon. Eased, however, in afternoon and evening after two more poultices and fomentations had been applied, so am just writing this out while it is easy, as I have not felt like it before.

<u>Sunday 22nd</u>. Woke this morning feeling something awful. Had been tossing about since 11 P.M. last night, suffering the most excruciating pain; I think it is the worst night I have ever spent in all my life. Was very thankful when the old man came in to bathe it at 5:30. At 9:30 A.M. when old poultice was taken off, found my knee covered in discharge, and great deal more coming out on pressure. By George! I did feel thankful. Felt like shouting champagne drinks, only it appeared rather impractical. Still more discharge during the day. The old man syringed it in the evening with some diluted Condy's Fluid, to wash out any lymph which might remain. He is simply delighted at the result of his labours, and says he feels "quite proud of it," as well he might be. He says he would have refused £20 to have had it happen "that'll show you, Owen!" All the fellows too, have been coming in to see me, and to express their satisfaction at hearing that the turning point was passed. A tremendous lot more discharge shot out this evening. The old man pulled out with his fingers, two long thick pieces of stuff resembling cord, the being the very core of the abscess. The amount which has come from the interior of my knee is astounding. About half-a-pannikin without the least exaggeration.

Art in 1895

Three days later, (which of course was Christmas day), he had recovered to the point where he was able to put weight on his leg. A Doctor friend of mine says it's called Bursitis, and Dr Google says that it usually gets better on its own accord. Maybe not in the middle of the Southern Ocean with Victorian medicine! They would be rounding Cape Horn two weeks later!

Being cooped up with the same people for three months at a time must have been difficult; the more so because the safety of all on board depended on the competence and skill of those in charge. A modern management study would have fun with some of the relationships. Here is Art talking about ship management in February 1895, sailing northwards in the Atlantic, at about the latitude of the Azores.

> Monday 24th February 1895. Very dull overcast day, with slight rain I n morning. Wind dropped about 6 A.M. and then suddenly shifted round to the NW with a heavy squall. Old man gave the second mate the order to take the head yards for'ard to port, but to keep them well checked in; the second mate proceeded to obey (?) but let go the upper topsails, and both topgallant braces; directly the sails filled, away went the yards fore and aft, almost jerking the topmast off her. Away for'ard came the old man, and seizing the second ma te, laid him gently (?) on the deck, at the same time applying a few choice adjectives to that said individual's name. Then proceeded to trim the yards himself, while trimming the main, the second mate laughed impudently at him, and away went the old man at him again, as no man in this world could have helped under the circumstances. He then sent him to his room and kept the watch himself. Sent for me in the forenoon, and showed me an account of the affair which he had written in the official log, along with a description of the great trouble he had had all through the passage with the second mate, asking me if I did not think it all correct and perfectly true, and which I fully endorsed. In afternoon, in the presence of second mate, ma tes, two A.B's, and myself, he read it over again, and we, as witness es, had to sign it. Mr. Johannsen was then sent to his room and told that he was to be treated as a saloon passenger for the remainder of the voyage, and that no more duty would be required of him. In re plying to the accusation, Mr. Johannsen denied letting them go, say-

-ing that he <u>did</u> take a turn with them. Wind hauled right round to the Nor'ard, and blew pretty stiff all day, moderating in the dog watch; making 10 knots E. Went about ship at 8 P.M. Heading NNW, and gradually coming up to her course again, NE 1/2 E by comp.

Art must have been liked and trusted by the Master of the ship, Captain Coles. No further management trouble occurred; they were nearly home.

<u>Saturday 7th</u>. Wind moderated greatly in middle watch, then shifted to the NNW and freshened a bit. Braced the yards round to port, and set foresail and upper topsails at 2 A.M. Passed <u>Beachy Head</u> about 3 A.M. <u>Dungeness</u> at 7:15. Put in our number, this being our first station to report at. Took pilot aboard - all hands being called at 7 A.M. to back the main yard - and tug "Nubia" coming off, the old man bargained with him to take us up, in conjunction with the "Burma," for £70 and use their own wires. Proceeded up through the Downs, passing Dover at 10:30 A.M.

Mermerus under full sail. Painting by Spurling

5   Steam ships

In the Spring of 1896, Art returned to London on board the Mermerus. He had completed his apprenticeship, and on his return received his certificate enabling him to be the Second Mate of a ship. I assume that getting that involved passing an exam; there was a gap of just less than a month between the date the Mermerus arrived, the 27th March and the date on the certificate.

So where does he go now, to go on getting the sea experience he needs?

It seems that his father was involved again. Art's father, Arthur Robert Owen, had become master of the 'Koh I Nor' paddle steamer in 1892. During the summer months, she provided a popular tourist attraction on the River Thames. The trip from London to Margate down the river had been popular since 1815, but to coming of the railway in 1851 meant that the trade became one of outings during the summer, rather than a simple means of transport.

. Koh-i-Noor 1909. From the Mick Twyman collection

The Koh I Nor was built in Glasgow; 300 ft long, she introduced the concept of a full length promenade deck to the tourist trade on the Thames.

This meant, I suppose that passengers could do what we would understand as a 'Titanic' imitation, standing on the railings right at the front of the ship. They wouldn't have understood the reference, though; the Titanic herself wouldn't be launched for another 20 years!

There is actually another link to the Titanic story; in May 1892 the newly built Koh I Noor, on her way from Glasgow, where she was built, to London, hit rocks in poor weather close to St David's in West Wales. She was nursed up the adjacent Milford Haven to Neyland; when the tide went out they found that 20 ft of her bow was crumpled up. Fortunately, she was built with watertight bulkheads throughout the ship which proved their worth.

She was on her way to London for the start of the tourist season, but carrying passengers with a crumpled bow doesn't inspire confidence. Apparently, she went back to Glasgow, the builders cut off the old bow section, and attached a brand new one; all in six days.

A voyage on a paddle steamer must have been a very enjoyable way of spending a summer afternoon. She could do 19 ½ knots; about 22 mph. Slow for a car, but quite fast for a boat! Standing on the promenade deck must have been a windy experience! The Koh I Noor went on doing the trip down the Thames in the summer season all the way through to the outbreak of the First World War.

She was so successful on the run from London to Harwich, that a close sister ship, the Royal Sovereign, was ordered for the 1893 season. So on the 20th May 1896, clutching his shiny new certificate, Art became the Second Mate on the Royal Sovereign.

Being on the Royal Sovereign must have felt so different from being on the Mermerus; no Southern Ocean gales; home every night for tea (well, maybe a little later); nice dry bed to sleep in!

Records that have survived suggest that there was a continuous low level war between the owners of the different sorts of vessels using the Thames. The Koh I Noor and the Royal Sovereign would have gone hammering down the River at 20 miles an hour, but these were quite big ships, and however sleek the hull shape, they generated quite a wake; and when that hit the barges also using the river, that resulted in everything being shaken up and down. There were a string of complaints made by 'lightermen' working on the River (who thought that 5 miles an hour was an entirely respectable speed for everyone) about the paddle steamers 'racing'; which of course they probably were; but proving which wave from which ship actually did the damage was another matter!

Art didn't keep a log for this period, but we know that he was working on the Royal Sovereign from May 1896 until the middle of September, and then did a week in the same role on the Koh I Noor. Maybe someone was off on the sick. It all counted towards time at sea for his qualifications.

There is a reference in Art's log to his father, Arthur Robert Owen. In 1894 he was appointed Captain of the company's new paddle steamer, the Marguerite. She was bigger and better again; 350 ft long, with a design limit of 3000 passengers. She was again built on the Clyde, at Glasgow. At this point Art is about to start his second voyage in the Mermerus.

> Saturday 2nd June 1894. Received sailing orders for Tuesday. Went aboard with Dad and saw Capt. Coles, who told me to join on Thursday.
>
> Sunday 3rd. Went with Ma, saw Dad off to Scotland by the 8:50 from Euston, and bade him goodbye.

'La Marguerite' was probably almost finished by now; she would have had sea trials to check that everything worked as it should, and then would have sailed south. On 16th June, when he was at sea in the Mermerus, Art records in his log that she should at least, have started service on the Thames that day.

> Saturday 16th June. Wore ship 8 bells, morning watch. Overhauled fore brace blocks, also fore and main topsail blocks (brace). Weather very warm, with very little wind, sometimes falling to dead calm. Averaged about 3 knots. Set in very foggy towards evening, with heavy Scotch mist. (Fog) horn underway. Paintwork work, brass cleaned, etc. for Sunday. "Marguerite's" first trip. Very wet all night. Lat. 46° 07' N, Long. 8° 04' W.

By this time, he was in the Bay of Biscay, close to the north western corner of Spain.

La Marguerite must have been something else as a paddle steamer. She was built specifically to take day trip passengers from London to Boulogne in

Four generations of the Owen family, taken in about 1909.

Left back is Arthur Robert Owen; right back Arthur Newton Owen. Seated is, I think, Ann Owen, Arthur Robert's mother, born about 1820, and on her lap is my father, Albert James Arthur Owen, who lived until 1997. Between them, therefore, the four people in this photo cover 177 years!

northern France. She was very popular but apparently not very profitable! By all accounts she got through an enormous amount of coal; and of course she only did the trip during the summer season, so couldn't give a massive return on the investment involved in building her.

A model of 'La Marguerite' in Liverpool Museum

One of her moments of glory, when captained by Arthur Robert Owen, was when she was hired by a certain Mr Thomas Cook to take people to inspect the Royal Navy ships gathered in the Solent for the Naval Review of 1897. There were 1300 ticket holders on board, and they didn't stint themselves; the team of chefs on board (145 of them) served a total of 5000 meals, including 800 lobsters and 5 hundredweight of salmon. What on earth does ¼ ton of salmon look like? Apparently there was a special catering train from London, just to carry the food!

This must have been a grand affair; it's also notable as the occasion when Charles Parsons demonstrated his steam turbine driven boat, the Turbinia, by streaking through the naval fleet at 34 knots. La Marguerite was no slouch, being certainly capable of 21 knots, but steam turbines were clearly the future.

Later in her career, she carried troops from Southampton to Le Havre in France. Over the course of the First World War, she carried over 360,000 troops to France, and covered 65,000 miles in the process. I suspect they didn't get the same level of catering!

One of the pieces of paper that has slipped through time and which has been digitised by somebody is a record of the numbers of troops that were carried across to Le Havre in the first World War. On May 6th in 1916, 6 troopships, including La Marguerite, docked in Le Havre, carrying a grand total of 114 officers, 3700 other ranks, and 1100 horses. All could have been in the front line within days; the battle of the Somme started six weeks later.

When she was broken up in 1925, the ship's bell was apparently presented to the HQ of the City of London Rifles, who were the first regiment to have been carried to the war in France on board her. The bell is now kept in St Sepulchure's church in Holborn in London.

So Art was Second Mate of the Royal Sovereign for most of the summer of 1896, shuttling up and down the Thames. Where does he go next?

The answer is New York! From the 24th October 1896, to the 12th November 1897, he was third mate of the 'Mohawk', a steamship operating between London and New York.

I should say that we know these dates with exactness because each time he finished working on a ship the Captain would sign a slip of paper that recorded his length of service and his conduct. Art kept these religiously, as you would expect; they are the evidence of his experience. All of them (as far as we know) have survived in a file that Art kept. His time on the Mohawk was a bit odd, in that after each return trip from London to New York he was discharged, only to be re-hired again within days. Maybe the company didn't have to pay him for the gap in between voyages; or maybe it simply didn't count as time at sea. So we know that Art did 11 transatlantic trips between October 1896 and November 1897.

I guess he got the third mate job (though he had a Second Mate certificate) because this was the first steam ship of any size that he had worked on. The Mohawk was 3,645 tons; more than twice the size of the Mermerus.

She had been built by Harland and Wolff in Belfast in 1892. She was 445 feet long and was capable of a speed of 13 knots, driven by the triple expansion steam engines that were making life so difficult for sailing ships like the Mermerus. She was one of four sister ships built for the Elder Dempster

(H.)—Complete List of Testimonials and full Statement of Service from first going to Sea, or from date of present Certificate.

No. of Testimonials	Ship's Name	Rig	Tonnage	Port of Registry and Official No. of Ship	Capacity	Date of Commencement	Date of Termination	Length of Service (Years/Months/Days)	Trade in which employed	Remarks	Initials of Verifier
	"Mermerus"	Ship	1671	Greenock	App.	27/3/93	27/3/96	3 — —	F		
	Greenwich Hospital School				1st Cl.	2/7/88	1/9/92	1 — —			
	"Royal Sovereign"	F.A.	189	London 102763	2nd mte	13/5/96	24/9/96			2/3 of this H.F. time is here reckoned	
	"Kohinoor"		F.A. 275	London 99083	2nd mte	15/9/96	22/9/96	3 —			
	"Mohawk"		F.A. 3645	London 99066	3rd mte	24/10/96	29/1/97	— 9 5	F		
Additional time continues with above	"Mohawk"		F.A. 3645	London 99066	3rd mte	30/1/97	14/4/97	— 3 13			

Total Service at Sea — 5 3 18 / 8 / 5
Time served for which Official proof is now produced — 1 0 5
Time served for which no proof is produced —

(I.)—Declaration to be made by Candidate.

(TAKE NOTICE. Any person who makes, or procures to be made, or assists in making, any false representation for the purpose of obtaining for himself or for any other person a Certificate of Competency shall be guilty of a Misdemeanor, and will render himself liable to heavy penalties.)

I do hereby declare that the particulars contained in Divisions (A.), (B.), (C.), (D.) and (H.) of this Form are correct and true to the best of my knowledge and belief; and that the PAPERS enumerated in Division (H.) and sent with this Form are true and genuine documents, given and signed by the persons whose names appear on them. I further declare that the Statement (H.) contains a true and correct account of the whole of my services without exception.

And I make this declaration conscientiously believing the same to be true.

Dated at London this 30th day of July 1897

Signed in the presence of the Superintendent of the Mercantile Marine Office.

A. Owen
Signature of Candidate
25 Annandale Rd. Greenwich
Present Address

This is the certificate that Art submitted to The Board of Trade in July 1897, as evidence of his experience, leading, hopefully, to his First Mate's certificate. It shows the time he spent in the Mermerus, Royal Sovereign, Kohinoor and the Mohawk, as well as the year he could claim from being a model student at the Royal Hospital School. It looks as if filling in a form in 1897 was just as complicated as doing it in 2024!

Line. All four were chartered by the Atlantic Transport Line, and were used on the London to New York service. In October 1896 the lease arrangement ended and the ships were purchased outright. They must have been making money. We know from the certificates kept by Art that each return trip, including time for loading and unloading, took about a month, so effectively the four ships must have been able to operate a weekly service between London and New York. There was a total lack of imagination by someone in naming the ships; Mohawk, Manitoba, Massachusetts and Mobile!

Between 1890 and 1899 3.7 million people emigrated to the USA. Most of these came from Europe, and 70% of the total arrived in New York. I suppose that means that starting the transatlantic trip in London, rather than, say, Liverpool, makes sense; London is on the European side of the UK.

There were at least another two ships owned or leased by the company; in 1898 all of them were requisitioned by the United States government as transports for service in the Spanish-American war which started on April 21st. In that role the Mohawk (re-named the 'Grant') could carry 80 officers, 1000 men and 1000 horses. The war only lasted until the August of 1898, and we will come across the 'Mohawk' again in Art's wanderings. She was eventually scrapped in 1946.

6   The brig 'Messenger'

A model of the 'Messenger' made by Art.

Art has done a stint on the passenger trade between London and New York, in a steam ship. Where does he go next? His first step is to have Christmas 1897 off; he finishes in the Mohawk in November, and stays ashore until January. He may have been doing some exams, because in December he is awarded his 'First Mate's certificate.

His next ship seems a bit 'sublime to the ridiculous' but that may not be right. In January 1898 he became the mate (the only one; no first, second and third mates here) in a 220 ton brig called the 'Messenger'. Being called a brig means that she had two masts with square sails on both, and with 'fore and aft' sails between the masts and rigged out onto a bowsprit above the bows of the ship. She had been built in South Shields on the Tyne in 1862, was registered in Yarmouth, and was owned, at the time Art was working on her, by a company in London. She probably had a crew of no more than 10. She was engaged in the coastal trade; i.e. between ports in Britain. She could probably go almost anywhere.

We don't know much about her, but we do have a model of the right sort of ship, made by Art, with '1898' written on the bottom of the hull: so it seems a fair bet that that is the 'Messenger'. It's actually a very well travelled model; it's been to California and back, so has been a lot farther than the original ship!

In Art's lifetime, and for a long while before, there was a difference between coastal trade and foreign trade; basically you didn't have to pay tax on goods in the coastal trade, but you did if the goods were coming from or going to a port abroad; so that is where and why you get smuggling!

The authorities kept a careful check, as far as they could, on trade between one port and another on the English coast; had what had left arrived, or had some been sneaked across the Channel when they weren't looking? Some of the books of these records have survived for particular ports, so people have been able to do research on what goods were carried, and the ships that carried them.

The same difference shows up in the qualification of the captain of a ship; you had a 'Master's ticket' for coastal trade, but an 'Extra Master' for foreign trade.

These days we automatically assume that any trade in a ship is between the UK and a foreign country, but it turns out that that is quite a recent idea.

I'd heard of the trade of coal from Newcastle to London, but I had really no idea of its extent. Research carried out by someone at the University of Cambridge has identified 17 major ports between London and the Scots border, all of which could have taken a ship the size of the Messenger, plus a host of smaller ones. On top of that you've got river and canal systems; too small for the Messenger, but they would have taken barges into which her cargo could have been transhipped. So the idea of someone at a factory in Oxford ordering a load of coal from Newcastle and having it delivered mostly by sea and river is entirely possible; and it was probably the cheapest way of doing it.

It does seem to have been something of a seasonal trade, at least for sailing ships; maybe the weather in the winter just got too unfriendly. People would have had to stockpile coal in the summer to last them through the winter.

In Britain we are just outside living memory of the beginnings of motorised road transport. I can remember our Dad (born in 1907) saying that he remembers his uncle (one of Art's brothers) having the first car in Gravesend, where he grew up; (cue sounds of antique car horn!) so in the time we are talking about with Art at the tail end of the 19th century, there are no cars, no lorries,

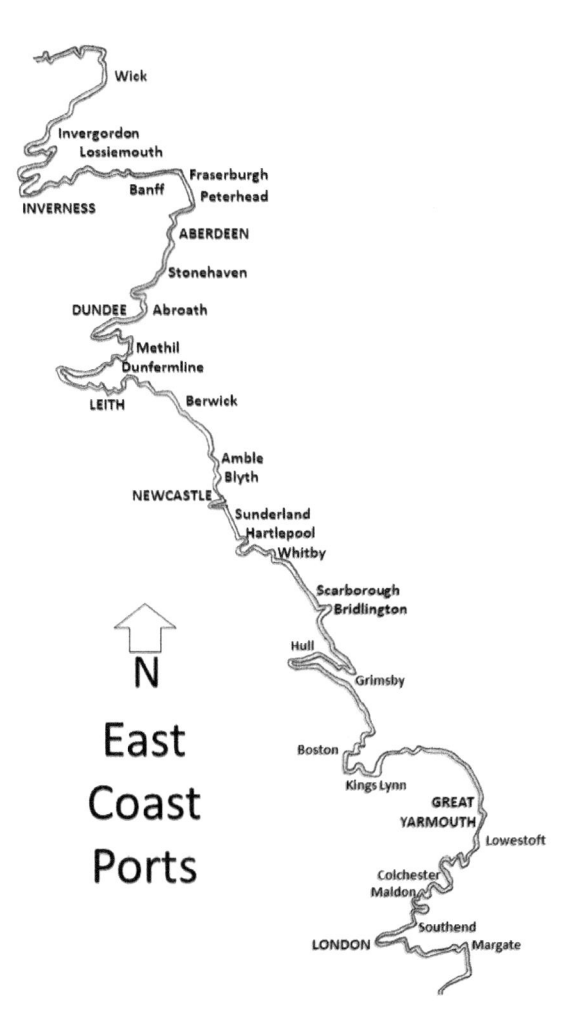

East Coast Ports

43

no main roads (why have a main road when everything is still pulled by a horse?) and no Motorways or Freeways!

The major consumer of coal from Tyneside must have been London. Every house had coal fires, all the way through to the middle of the 20th century. We've heard of London 'Smogs', of which the worst was in 1952. Given particular weather conditions smoke would mix with fog, and the result brought everything to a halt; particularly because it was difficult to breathe. There is an episode in the 'Crown' series where the sub plot is the death of an aide to Winston Churchill who stepped out in front of a bus and was killed; she simply didn't see the lights of the bus through the smog.

Campaigning against the use of coal is therefore not a new thing; the 'Clean Air Act' of 1956 was an early start to the process in Britain. The nearest coal field, by sea to London was the area around Newcastle; so there must have been a continuous stream of ships coming down the East coast.

This coastal trade answers another question from my family tree: my Mother's grandfather, one Aaron Hurrell, was born in Maldon in Essex. He married a nice girl from South Shields; how did they get together? The answer of course is that he went to sea in the coastal trade. Eventually he got his Extra Master's ticket and became the captain of a ship trading into the Black Sea, but that's another story.

I'd assumed that when the railways really got going in Britain in the 1850's they would have taken all the trade that used to be carried along the coast in ships; but apparently the reverse was true.

One study of the trade into and out of ports in North eastern Scotland has said that transport by sea was, in 1896, considerably cheaper than having the same goods carried on a train. The train was more reliable, so I guess that if you had perishable goods then that was the way to go; but if you were transporting coal, or grain, or timber, or any other bulk cargo, where it didn't matter if it arrived tomorrow or in two days time, then go for a ship.

When we looked at Art's travels on the Mermerus, we came to the conclusion that sailing ships were just about competitive with steam powered vessels. The same seems to be true here; the coastal trade was carried by a mixture of both steam powered and sailing vessels.

Some of that competitiveness was probably due to the much lower building and running costs of a sailing ship. The 'Messenger' was built in 1862 and was clearly still going strong in 1898. In fact she shows up on the 'Mercantile Navy list' until 1921; 59 years later.

If you had a truck, these days, that was still running happily and competitively 36 years after it came out of the factory, let along 50 years, you would be well pleased! The return on the original investment must have been quite impressive. In the third quarter of the 19th century, those who owned the ships that sailed out of Aberdeen were making a return of 5% or 6% per annum on average. Between 1866 and 1896 the number of vessels using Peterhead harbour in Scotland had grown by 25%.

Coal would have been one of the staple cargoes. Yarmouth, where the 'Messenger' was registered, was home to a big seasonal fishing fleet, catching herring. At the end of the century these boats were gradually changing from sail to steam power, which of course would have needed coal. There is a certain irony in this coal being brought to Yarmouth by a sailing ship, but it's quite possible!

Art didn't leave any record of the travels of the 'Messenger' except for one cryptic comment on the 9th January 1899, when he was sailing southwards in the Atlantic on board another ship altogether.

> Joined "Messenger" twelve months ago today. "Oh!, the memories of that night." Thank heaven she's done with.

Art's time in the 'Messenger' finished at the end of October 1898. He had three weeks off and then was appointed as the First Mate of the Barque, 'Peri' sailing out of London; this time not in the coastal trade but anywhere in the world that a cargo was to be carried. He didn't come home for two years.

7   The voyage of the 'Peri' to Fremantle

The Barque 'Peri' had been built in 1868, and lasted until 1907. She was 212 ft long and had been built by a shipyard in South Shields. In 1877 she had been lengthened, and may at that point have been converted from a 'ship' rig (square sails on all three masts) to a barque: square sails on the forward two masts.

She made at least three voyages between London and Fremantle, in 1897, 1898 and (with Art on board) in 1900.

I think, before we talk about the wanderings of the 'Peri', I ought to mention Art's home life. This is 1899; Art is 21, but as far as we know, is still living at home between voyages. His father, Arthur Robert, is now the Assistant Superintendent of the 'Foreign Cattle Market' in Deptford, which was owned by the London City Corporation.

This was presumably one of those jobs that simply ceased to exist when the refrigeration of meat became possible; until then, cattle had to be imported live, and presumably held in a market until sold on. It sounds, yet again, that it was who you knew that was important; the Superintendent of the market, a Mr George Philcox, had given our Art a very nice gold pocket watch on his 21st birthday, the year before. Must have been a family friend!

The family had moved to a house in Annadale Road, in Greenwich, which is still there. They went to church at Maze Hill Chapel in Greenwich, which is not still there; it was closed in the 1970's.

One of the other families in the church were the Batchelors; father a 'Chemical Merchant' according to the 1901 census, but in the 1911 census he was at particular pains to note that he was also the organist at the Maze Hill chapel.

The Batchelors had a daughter, Florence, a year younger than Art. It's quite possible that they had known each other for years. Judging by the entries he makes in his diary of his journey in the 'Peri' he was very fond of her; maybe even engaged to her; certainly the families thought of them that way.

Enough of this sitting around at home, chatting up young ladies; there is a voyage to undertake! Back to the Peri.

This was a smaller ship; about half of the tonnage of the Mermerus. Probably slower, run on less money and going anywhere where there was a cargo to be carried. On this voyage, she actually sailed to Australia, then across the Pacific round Cape Horn, to the east coast of S America, then to Cape Town, back to New Zealand, and then round the Horn (again!) and back to the UK. The whole voyage took 2 years.

They left London, headed for Australia, on the 25th November, but progress was very slow. By the 27th they were at anchor off Deal, Kent, waiting for a favourable wind. On the 28th, which is day three of the journey it rained all day, with light winds.

> Tuesday 29th November. **(day four)** About 10 p.m. it came on to blow a regular howler from the NNE with heavy squalls and rapidly increasing sea. Tried twice to get anchor, but were unable to get the link. Not deeming it prudent for ship to cast inshore, there being great danger of ship going ashore before paying off, the old man, after consulting with all hands, decided the safest course was to slip the cable, which we did at 30 fathoms. Set all heavy sail and proceeded through Downs.

So they were unable to hoist the anchor, and instead let the cable and the anchor go. It's probably still down there!

If they were that close to the land, it must have been a very hairy moment to let go of the anchor, (at which point the ship is being blown backwards) and then to turn her so that she is running before the wind, down the Channel. Art is being very nonchalant about the 'not deeming it prudent' bit; it must have been really quite scary!

At 11 a.m. the next day, **day five**, the wind had shifted round to the West North West, a headwind from the point of a ship trying to make her way down channel. He makes three references to sighting Portland Bill, which is a prominent headland on the coast of Dorset, at different times, showing that despite tacking to and fro across the Channel, the ship was making almost no headway.

I suppose if you are used to sailing, then a lot of Art's experience sounds normal; but bear in mind that this is in a ship with no engine, no radar, no 'sat nav'; making the comment about siting Portland Bill depends on the guy on the bow of the ship keeping a lookout, the weather being clear enough to see it in time, and furthermore recognizing this headland for what it is. There must have been discussions; is that Portland Bill, or the Isle of Wight, or Start Point; where are we?

> Friday 2nd. **(day seven)** Wind gradually increased to fresh gale by noon with heavy squalls and rapidly increasing sea. Reduced sail bit by bit until under lower topsails. Ship labouring and plunging heavily and shipping heavy water. 8 p.m. weather moderated somewhat, but sea still very heavy.

> Saturday 3rd. **(day eight)** Strong Westerly wind with heavy gusts of wind and rain. Sea still running very high and making the old girl kick her heels about. Shipped rather less water. Set foresail, fore and main reefed topsails, jib and spanker. Pity we didn't stop at Deal. Wore ship again at 4 a.m. and 4 p.m.

Wearing a ship; from Villiers

Wearing and tacking are two different ways of changing direction; wearing was probably safer in a strong wind, but both mean losing some ground.

> Sunday 4th. **(day nine).** Same old thing again. Strong wind from West south west and dirty overcast weather and rain squalls every five minutes. Wore ship only three times at 4 a.m. and 2 and 6 p.m. I'm sick of hearing the word "wear ship."

> Monday 5th. **(day ten!)** Fresh to strong wind from West south west all day, with misty squalls of rain and a lumpy sea still

running. Wore ship three times at 4 a.m. Portland Bill bore North westerly. Oh! for an easterly wind.

They are still in the same area, on day fourteen, four days later. Nine further days passed, in which they suffered the effects of five successive gales, and having made it as far down channel as Devonshire on the 6th, they were back close to the Isle of Wight; further east than Portland Bill. As First Mate, Art would have been second in command of the ship, taking charge of one of the two 'watches' into which the crew was divided. Wearing ship in heavy

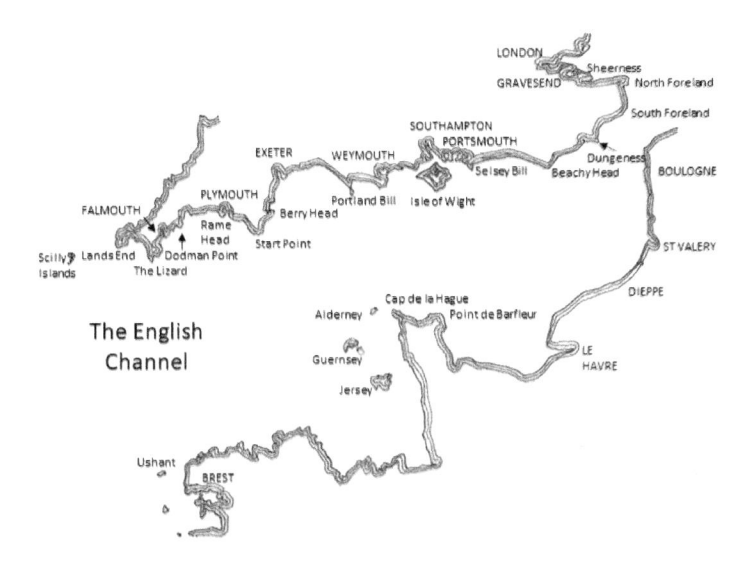

Map of The English Channel showing locations including London, Gravesend, Sheerness, North Foreland, South Foreland, Southampton, Portsmouth, Selsey Bill, Dungeness, Beachy Head, Boulogne, Exeter, Weymouth, Isle of Wight, Portland Bill, Plymouth, Berry Head, Falmouth, Rame Head, Start Point, Dodman Point, The Lizard, Lands End, Scilly Islands, St Valery, Dieppe, Cap de la Hague, Alderney, Point de Barfleur, Guernsey, Jersey, Le Havre, Ushant, Brest.

weather would have needed all of the crew, so no-one would have got much rest. His prayers for an easterly wind were not answered; by the 16th December, they were still close to the Lizard, a prominent headland in Cornwall. It had taken them three weeks to get to this point.

In part because of this, the 'Peri' made an appallingly slow journey to her initial destination, Freemantle, in Western Australia. Her eventual arrival was reported in the local paper after a voyage of 151 days; she arrived on the 26th April 1899. Compare that with the 89 days taken by the Mermerus to get to Melbourne (a longer journey) in 1893. In that time, of course, with no radio on board, no one in the outer world would have known where they were, if indeed the ship was still afloat at all.

When they did get to Freemantle, Art found 24 letters from home waiting for him!

Three themes emerge from Art's diaries of this voyage; his frustration at the lack of progress, the fact that he was clearly missing 'Flo' as he calls her, quite badly, and his frustration at the captain of the 'Peri'.

Here's some sample entries from his diary which illustrate all three. It doesn't look as if it's going to be a very happy voyage!

> Thursday 15<u>th</u> December 1898. At 6:30 a.m., having just got comfortably into my pew, all blessed hands called once more to wear ship, the wind having gone to NNW and then fallen calm. Felt about as sweet-tempered as I ever did in my life and all hands feeling about the same, especially my watch; the only one happy is the old man, who has been asleep since 8:30 last night, so doesn't mind turning out. I shall turn grey-headed if this lasts much longer. Set all sail on the other tack and headed West, making <u>quite</u> one knot per hour and one onion. The day turned out very fine - quite summer like. Hands doing odd jobs about decks. Wind very light towards night.
>
> <u>Friday 16th</u>. A regular T.R. sort of day. Light airs or calms with dense patches of wet mist and fog all day, sea smooth. 8 a.m. wore ship and <u>headed</u> Northwards - but this doesn't mean we went very far North. During afternoon passed the time feeling our way with the lead, making about 60 fathom each time, sandy bottom. We are three weeks out from London this morning, and are only just off the Lizard; which on ordinary occasions any vessel can do in 48 hours. This is bally awful.
>
> <u>Saturday 17th</u>. Today is dear old Flo's birthday; with all my heart I wish her many happy returns of the day, and everything else that's good in the future. Only wish I could have been at home today to wish it her personally, but it's not much good wishing out here. Have felt very dumpy all day, but guess I must buck up. Only hope I shall be home for her next one.

> The weather has been the same all day today, with dense fog nearly the whole time; the blessed tooter has been singing all day too, most cheering blessed row. Several steamers passed close, also windjammers. The best thing we can do is to cast lots and see who the Jonah is. 10 p.m. fog cleared up - fine night.

The voyage went on being slow, and he went on missing Flo.

He went on being frustrated by the Master of the ship, as well. When they were sailing from New Zealand towards London in the latter part of the voyage, the Master (and it's about a year before we find out that he is called Captain Clarkson!) wasn't very well with some sort of mystery illness, so Art was in full charge of the ship.

> <u>Tuesday, September 4 1900</u>
>
> Gale gradually moderated during the day, with fine clear weather. Sea still very heavy, but slowly decreasing. Squared away at 10.0 a.m. and set foresail and fore lower topsail. Upper topsails and reefed mainsail later. Wind moderating rapidly in afternoon; set all plain sail. Very heavy northerly swell, causing ship to roll heavily. The skipper has been laid up nearly a fortnight with sundry pains, imaginary or otherwise; whether or no, everybody knows it, but then he's the only man who <u>may</u> be ill aboard this ship. Anyhow I congratulate myself on the fact that I truly and honestly believe the ship to be at the very <u>least</u> 150 miles further ahead than she would have been had he been on deck!! Wind falling light towards midnight, and westering. Lat. 49° 50' S, Long. 136° 58' W.

The Master had been ill for 2 weeks at this point; it would be the end of September before he was well enough to take charge again, by which time they had rounded Cape Horn, and were heading home northwards in the Atlantic. Art was very pleased with his navigation skills!

Back to the speed, or lack of it, of the voyage. The speed of a ship is a function of the length of the ship; but you need to also consider the design of the ship, the weather they encounter and the ability of the Master to handle her properly. That's a lot of variables.

 The Mermerus regularly did the voyage to Melbourne, which is in the south-east corner of Australia, 1600 miles further than Fremantle in between 65-75 days, but on day 40 of the 'Peri's' voyage, she was still off Spain. By day 60, they were just about to cross the Equator. That starts to have all sorts of implications:

> Tuesday 24th January. 60 DAYS today - and NOT yet across the LINE. Oh, Harriet, I'm a-waiting! Holiday this day, as in all probability we should cross the line, although at noon we were still 18 miles North. Awfully hot again, with gentle breeze, first SSW, veering to SW by W in afternoon. Caught four fine dolphins with a hook and line and fed on them for tea. Couldn't be much fresher if you wanted them. Measured the water in tanks and found about 1,900 gallons left. Skipper put all hands on 3 quarts a day. This is lively! With this heat, a fellow wants about a gallon a day to drink, to say nothing of washing self and clothes. Oh, for a storm of rain for 4 hours. Wonderful life, this!!! Lat. 0° 18' N, Long. 23° 3' W.

Art makes the point that the weather would be wonderful, except for sailors on a windjammer. Finally, on the 29th January the wind becomes more consistent; they are in the South East Trade winds. But it's still terribly hot.

These winds are generally pushing them southwards, which is OK in principle, but they are reaching the point where they would want to be sailing eastwards, to pass to the south of the Cape of Good Hope; the southern point of the African continent. Finally on the 2th February, the wind starts blowing from the north West.

> Monday 20th February. Mod. to fresh NW wind all day, with very fine clear weather, though cloudy at times with moderate following sea. This is something like running the easting down - long may it last. Set up fore topmast rigging and other small jobs. Beautiful night. More like the trades weather. Lat. 34° 47' S, Long. 24° 57' W.

Reading Art's diary, the latitude figure he gives now stays roughly constant at about 36 degrees south; measured from the Equator. The longitude, the measure of distance that the ship is to the west of the Greenwich meridian (0 degrees; which in this part of the world is still to the west of South Africa) gets less and less. They are heading towards Australia, but they are still in the centre of the Atlantic. They do pass close to the isolated Island of Tristan da Cunha, which at least gives them a chance to check exactly where they were.

> Saturday 25th February Dull overcast weather with gale moderating rapidly, but wind gradually hauling after a quick shift from NW to WSW, to SW and South. At 5:30 a.m. Tristan da Cunha Island bore SSE 48 miles, but was only visible for a short time on account of thick mist and rain on horizon, according to 2nd mate. Passed Tristan da Cunha at 6 a.m. Settled into a very fine night, cloudless sky, but very little wind up to midnight. Lat. 36° 16' S, Long. 11° 41' W.
>
> Friday 3rd March. Crossed the Meridian of Greenwich today. Morning broke fine and clear with mod. breeze and fine clear weather. Set all sail gradually through the morning. Wind remained pretty steady all day from WSW, sky partially clouded. Heavy swell first part, moderating later. Rove new main buntlines. Shifted mizzen staysail and various small jobs. We are 14 weeks or 98 days from London today and NOT.YET.OFF.THE. CAPE. Flo dearie, how I do long to get a letter from you and hear all the news. I'm much afraid you'll have to wait some time yet before you get one from me, but never mind, old girl. There'll come time some day. Lat. 39° 30' S, Long. 0° 26' E.

By the 11th March, they have at last passed the Cape of Good Hope. They are further south; the Latitude figure is now 41 degrees, and the longitude figure is now increasing and labelled 'East': they are east of the Greenwich meridian.

> Saturday 11th. Rain, lightning, mist and other sundry luxuries cleared off at 3 a.m. followed by fine clear weather and light to moderate breeze. Set all sail. Cleaned ship in forenoon and knocked off at 11 a.m. Very fine weather throughout - more like trades in afternoon. Painted out my room - first coat. Night very fine indeed - quite light with stars, although no moon. What Ho! Passed the Cape of Good Hope at last this morning. 106 days – a record I guess. Lat. 41° 7' S, Long. 19° 5' E.

The seas to the south of 40 degrees S latitude are known as the Roaring Forties. The wind and therefore the waves have an almost un-interrupted run around the whole world, so the winds are strong, and the waves big.

> Friday 17th March. Moderate to light W to NW winds all day with clear cloudy weather and moderate swell. Hands chipping bulwarks, tarring rigging, etc. Very quiet day generally, ditto night. From 9 to 11 p.m. the water presented a most remarkable appearance being all of aglow; not ordinary phosphorescence, but for all the world as though we were on a sand bank with very little water under us and a sandy bottom. Most weird appearance, all hands remarking same. I remember it once before in "Mermerus," just before we got a tremendous blow. Hope it doesn't mean the same now. Lat. 41° 11' S, Long. 35° 53' W.
>
> Saturday 18th. Began with moderate breeze and fine clear weather with passing clouds. Commenced cleaning poop brightwork in morning. At 2 p.m. wind freshened, handed all light sail. At 8 p.m. increased to strong breeze with moderate increasing sea. Glass falling rapidly. At 9:30 increased rapidly to fresh gale. Called all hands (poor me below again) and shortened sail, and hove to under main topsail and mizzen. staysail. Main upper topsail blew to pieces in the buntlines before I could make it fast. By midnight, a strong gale and very high sea with squalls of hurricane force. "Alright for Sunday." Lat. 41° 15' S, Long. 38° 33' E.

The Peri had no radio, and therefore there was no way of telling anybody where they were. However there seems to have been an arrangement whereby if another ship passed them, they could ask for their position to be reported. When that ship reached port, they would send a message back to London to the effect that they had seen the 'Peri' at such and such a position, on such and such a date. This was then published in certain newspapers.

> Wednesday 29th March . Strong N-NW wind all day with heavy puffs and rain at times, and fine clear weather between; a sort of gale in penny numbers. At 9 a.m. N. Zealand Shipping Co. S/S Waiwera passed close under our stern, taking our name, so that they ought to

know where we are in three weeks' time anyhow. Expect they are studying the gazette at home, unless they have had a report. Have you looked with Daily News lately, Flo, old girl?; guess you'll be disappointed for some time to come yet. Just a year ago tonight since I sang "Jack's The Boy" at the choir concert at Maze Hill. Oh, law! - I wish I was there now instead of fighting the elements down here. Lat. 42° 50' S, Long. 57° 25' E.

It was going to be almost another month before they made it to Fremantle on the 26th April; 155 days from London.

Wednesday 26th April. Grand sleep last night! Feel a new man!!! Began with mod. S'ly wind and light rain squalls which cleared off at 10 a.m. and resulted in a lovely day; clear sky and smooth sea. Set down all sail, both royal yards and all heavy gear. Splendid day's work. Got letters off this afternoon. Hooray! We live! Got 24. Spent the evening reading them all through twice, and feel much more as though I still belonged to the world and some of the people in it. It is now 10:15 p.m. so here goes for a turn in. In Fremantle (Gage Roads).

The Barque 'Peri'. In Port Chalmers, New Zealand. Date unknown

London: left 25/11/1898
Arrived 26/11/1900

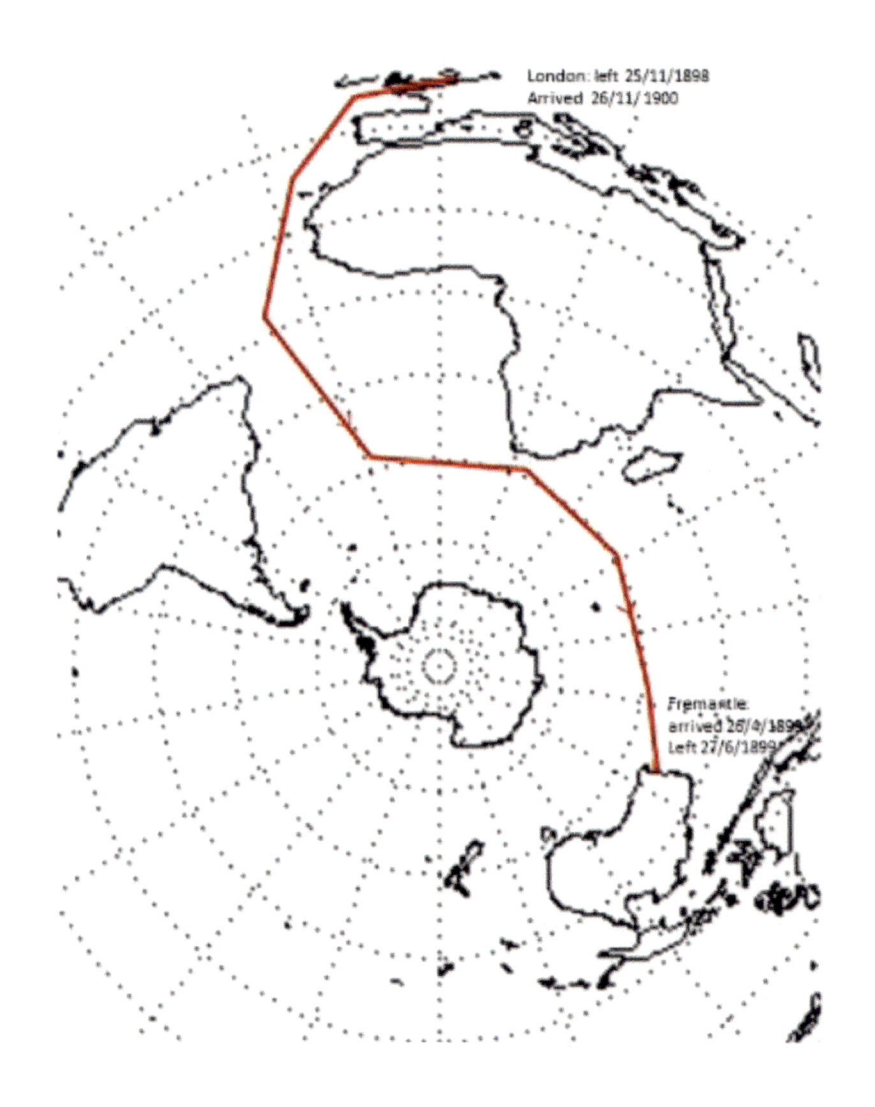

Fremantle:
arrived 26/4/1899
Left 27/6/1899

8   The voyage of the 'Peri':
Fremantle to Cape Town

Art's first impression of Fremantle wasn't great!

> "Went ashore in afternoon - came back very shortly. Fremantle - rotten, disgusting hole. Shan't trouble it much - thank heaven when we leave."

That was at the end of April; by the time they left, towards the end of June, his views had changed substantially!

> <u>Tuesday 27th June</u>. Sent out jibboom and set up all head gear, bent jibs, etc., and prepared generally for sea. Our last night in this port. Great weeping and wailing, etc. Jolly sorry to leave, my opinions about Fremantle have altered very considerably.

Spoiler alert; he has met a young lady! We'll find more about her later. He has also had his photo taken, inscribed 'Webb and Webb, Artist Photographers, High Street, Fremantle.

As far as we know, this is the only time he ever came here, so we can date it precisely: June 1899. Art is 22, and looks the master of his craft. He has written 'Your loving sailor boy, Art' across the corner; the only question is which young lady he is going to give it to!

The next stop for the 'Peri' is not far away; the port of Albany is just around the bottom left hand corner of Australia.

It's ironic that one of the most dangerous places for a sailing ship, indeed any ship, is close to shore. When you are in the open sea, it doesn't matter too much if the wind doesn't blow you where you want to go; but close to shore, a wind that blows you towards that shore is very dangerous.

The first part of the voyage was straightforward. They left Fremantle, towed out by a tug on the 29th June; by the evening of the 30th they had sited Cape Leeuwin, which is effectively the bottom left hand corner of Australia, and had turned eastward. But the wind, which had been from the north east and east, allowing them to sail southwards, was now in the wrong direction for them to sail to the east.

> Saturday 1st July. Begins with fresh breeze and fine clear weather, with choppy sea. Wind between NE-NNE. We are now jammed up in it, although still jogging along the land, which was well visible all along to the Nor'ard. At 9:20 a.m. got a cross bearing. White Capped Rocks bearing N 1/2 W and Chatham Island (East end) NE by E 1/2 E (true). Soon after noon, wind freshening and gradually backing to the ENE. Forced to stand off. This is hard luck; the glass continues rising too. By 10 p.m. wind increased to mod. gale and squally. Shortened sails to two lower topsails gradually between 5 and 10 p.m. Rough sea. Here we are again! All a-blowing. At midnight wore ship and stood North.

So initially they can hold their course; then the wind moves from NE towards East, and they have to steer away from the land. At midnight, not wanting to get too far south, they turned the ship and steered north. The 'glass' or barometer is almost one of those instruments that has been confined to history,

The voyage of the 'Peri': Fremantle to Albany, 1899

but to Art it was the best indicator of what weather was coming over the horizon towards him. It's been replaced on land at least, by the mobile phone!

These conditions continue for the next two days; a balancing act between not getting too close to the land, or getting too far away to the south. Suddenly, then, at 1.30pm on the 4th, the wind changes direction, and blows from the south west. By 8.00pm it had freshened to gale force, and had swung around to the south, pushing them towards the shore.

> <u>Wednesday 5th July</u>. Continued blowing a fresh Southerly gale with terrible squalls of wind and rain. Passed a rather anxious night, we being not far from a lee shore and drifting there almost bodily; unable to do anything with the heavy sea. Skipper right clean off his chump - talking like a maniac. Got a star on Meridian at 4 a.m., however, and found we still had good sea room, so guess all's well yet. At daybreak, land in sight. Continued blowing hard all day, but with finer weather and squalls as frequent and heavy. At 1 p.m. wind inclined to freshen and appearances dirty. We decided to run for Albany and chance it, as squared away set foresail and reefed topsails. 7:30 p.m. Breaksea Point in sight ahead. Shaped course accordingly to clear Maude Reef. 9:30 Bald Head abeam. 10:30 passed between Breaksea Island and Bald Head and entered King George's Sound. 11 p.m. clewed up all sail and let go the mudhook in 7 fathom with 60 fathom starboard anchor. Thank God we are here safe after all. Set anchor watch.

Breaksea Point and Bald Head are either side of the entrance to Albany. They have made it!

Art comments that Albany has a superb harbour, and looks to be a very nice town. After that, his next diary entry is on 18th July. They have finished loading their cargo, and are ready for sea.

He doesn't say what their cargo is; it seems to be no concern of his! What would someone want to be shipped from South West Australia to Buenos Aires, which is where they are going next? Actually if we leap forward a month in his diary, he refers to the ship being loaded with timber. Who would pay for timber to be carried from Australia to South America remains a mystery!

By the 28th July (which is of course the winter in this part of the world), they are back in the Roaring Forties; Latitude 43 degrees south, and roughly midway between Albany, on the west side of the continent, and Tasmania on the east. The winds are generally from the west, which is what you would expect, and what they want, but regularly they are so strong that they have to 'heave to'.

> <u>Friday 28th</u>. Wind gradually increased in violence and sea heavier. At 4 a.m. blowing strong from NW by W with dirty looking weather. Handed foresail, fore topsail and main topgallant. Glass falling rapidly. Continued to run under short canvas until 11 a.m. then forced to heave to under main topsail and mizzen staysail and spanker on account of very high sea running. Continued blowing a fresh to strong gale all night, with very heavy squalls of hurricane force and a mountainous sea running. Kept oil going on weather bow.
>
> Lat. 44° 44' S, Long. 131° 9' E.

So they have been running, with the wind behind the ship, but the size of the waves makes that dangerous. They swing round, so that the ship takes the waves on her bow; the mizzen staysail and the spanker (both set on the rearmost mast), keep the ship in that position. Oil into the water calms the waves (slightly!)

It wasn't blowing a gale all the time, though there seems to have been a lot; but from the 9th to the 19th August they had fine weather. These days we are used to weather forecasts informed by satellites; my son in law has an 'ap' on his phone that tells him exactly what the weather is going to do in the next hour. All Art had was the 'mark 1 eyeball' and a barometer.

> <u>Sunday 20th August</u>. Light wind and fine weather all day; heavy swell working up from SW and glass falling rapidly; we're evidently pretty close to something hot. Fell 17-100 this afternoon. Reduced sail to lower topsails and staysails. 7 p.m. wind still increasing, hove to on port tack under main topsails, mizzen staysail, and spanker.
> Lat. 46° 29' S, Long. 169° 4' W.

Adjusting the sails set to fit with what the weather was doing was an almost continuous process. It's not unusual for Art to record three or four changes in the sails set in a given day; each responding to what the weather was throwing at them. A barque like the 'Peri' had square sails on the fore and main masts, then 'fore and aft' sails on the third, mizzen, mast, and more fore and aft sails set between the masts and between the foremast and the bowsprit. On each of the two square sailed masts the sails, from the bottom up, were a 'course' (also known as the foresail or the mainsail), a lower and upper topsail, a topgallant sail and then, smallest at the top, a 'royal'.

Minimum sail in a gale was a lower fore topsail and the 'spanker' which was the large sail set to the rear of the mizzen mast.

The volume of Art's diary which started with their departure from Fremantle ends at the end of August 1899, half way across the Pacific, at Lat. 46° 35' S, Long. 151° 4' W. which puts them 2000 miles from New Zealand, 2000 miles from Antarctica, and 3200 miles from Cape Horn. They are basically a long way from anywhere! They have travelled 4500 miles since they left Albany, and it's taken them 44 days to do it; an average of just over 100 miles per day. We don't know what happened to Art's next diary; if he kept one it's become separated from the rest at some point in the last 120 years.

The crew of the 'Peri'. Art is in the front row, 2nd from left.

The voyage of the Peri; 1899-1900 Fremantle to Cape Town.

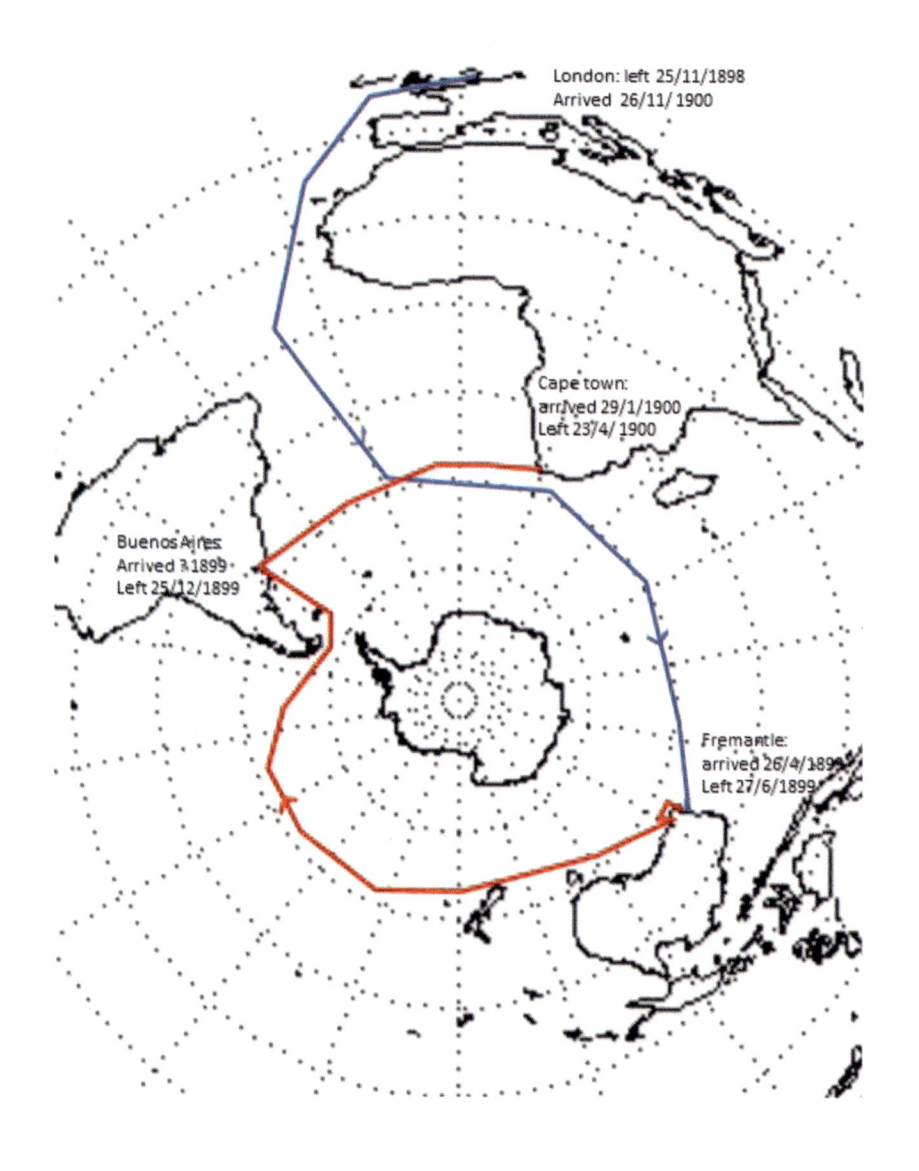

London: left 25/11/1898
Arrived 26/11/1900

Cape town:
arrived 29/1/1900
Left 23/4/1900

Buenos Aires
Arrived ?1899
Left 25/12/1899

Fremantle:
arrived 26/4/1899
Left 27/6/1899

The next volume that we have starts on Sunday December 24th in 1899. They are about to leave Buenos Aires; we don't know how long they have been there, but if they kept up the same '100 miles a day' average over the 4700 miles left of the journey they would have been in Buenos Aires at about the end of October. It was either a very slow voyage or they have been sitting in port for some time!

It's difficult to know how cargoes for a ship like the 'Peri' were organized; they have just carried timber from Australia to Buenos Aires, but it's clearly not Art's place, as first mate, to negotiate a cargo for the next leg of the voyage. I suspect that the owner's agent in London did the negotiating. But the ship would remain in a given port until something was agreed, or might sail somewhere 'in ballast' without a cargo if there was really nothing to be had. The next port they visit after Buenos Aires is Cape Town, in South Africa; from a comment that Art makes about unloading there, it sounds as if they were carrying wheat.

So on the 28th December 1899, the 'Peri' sailed from Buenos Aires. There was a slight pause when the wind changed to blow straight up the channel; they dropped anchor. The next day they got going again. On the 31st, the wind gradually freshened, and there was heavy lightning; Art calls it a 'beautiful start for the New Year; what you might call coming in with honours. Spliced the main brace at 8 bells. Goodbye to 1899. May this time next year see me at home'.

> Monday, January 1 - 4 days out
>
> A Happy New Year to everybody! - especially ourselves, very much so!!
>
> At 1.0 a.m. fell dead calm, then wind suddenly sprang up from SW, falling away again soon after, and continuing to come in strong puffs with heavy rain, lightning and thunder throughout the morning. Spent a most <u>enjoyable</u> watch from midnight to 4.0 a.m., seeing the New Year in under delightful conditions. At 10.0 a.m. a steady breeze setting in from South, set all heavy canvas up to noon. The weather very unsettled and threatening in appearance. At 6.0 p.m. increased to a moderate gale and shifted to SE.

Handed upper topsails. At 9.0 p.m. (my watch on deck) a heavy thunderstorm burst over ship, with forked and chain lightning all over heavens and continuous rain, with darkness that you could almost feel.

St. Elmo's Fire showing at the trucks and yardarms - a most rare and peculiar sight only met with at sea, I believe, and that only on rare occasions. Towards midnight the wind gradually moderated and hauled to East; wore ship 'round to port tack on my own, skipper being bad with rheumatics.

Lat. 36° 41' S, Long. 54° 9' W.

The weather cleared.

Wednesday, January 3 - 6 days out

Fine clear weather all day with a steady SW wind and light passing clouds. Moderate quarterly sea. A really perfect day for sailing; even the old "Peri" has forgotten herself and been going for all she's worth, logging a steady 9 knots all the latter part of the day. Kept all sail on until 11.0 p.m.; when extra strong puff setting in, furled mainsail and royals.

Lat. 37° 12' S, Long. 50° 23' W.

They are sailing along the same line of latitude, travelling due east. The figure Art records for the longitude decreases each day; 10 days out, Long. 42 degrees, 15 days out, Long. 30 degrees, 20 days out, Long. 16 degrees. On day 21 they crossed the course they had followed on their way out from the UK, on the 25th February the year before.

Thursday, January 18th – 21 days out

Moderate to fresh breeze all day from WSW-W and fine clear weather. Passing clouds and moderate following swell. All suitable sail set. Hands scrubbing brightwork. At 7.0 p.m. this evening passed Tristan da Cunha. 18 miles dist., but not visible on account of heavy cloud banks. Weather very fine up to midnight.

Lat. 36° 39' S, Long. 13° 29' W.

Sunday, January 21 - 24 days out

> Fresh to moderate W'ly wind all day with fine clear weather greater part, clouding over at times. Rough following sea and long swell. This is certainly grand going and no mistake, even for a far smarter ship than the "Peri." Since leaving B.A. we have averaged 119 miles per day, or about 5 knots per hour. Certainly an excellent record! Long may she keep it up!! Continued a moderate breeze to midnight accompanied by light patches of drizzling rain. Swell moderating.
>
> Lat. 36° 40' S, Long. 2° 49' W.

On January 22nd, 25 days out, they crossed the Meridian; they are 6000 miles due south of Art's home in Greenwich, London. They are starting to get close to Cape Town, and start preparing the ship. Anchors are connected to cables, ready to be used; the paintwork on the ship is being smartened up. On January 29th they sighted Table Mountain, behind Cape Town.

Monday, January 29 - 32 days out

> Gentle to moderate SW wind all day with beautifully fine clear weather. At 4.30 p.m. made out Table Mountain ahead, it being just daylight; making the land just as we expected. Chronometers being correct to a mile. Shaped course accordingly. Rose the land rapidly during forenoon. Cape of Good Hope light abeam at 10.0 a.m. 1.30 p.m. Lion's Head Mountain abeam, the summit of this mountain bearing a remarkable resemblance to a crouching lion, and being most appropriately named. 2.30 p.m. Green Point Light abeam. 3.30 p.m. entered Table Bay. There being no pilot, brought ship to wind. 4.0 p.m. Harbour boat came off and instructed us to proceed up bay. 5.0 p.m. let go anchor with 45 fathom on starboard anchor in 7 fathom water. Set anchor watch. Night fine with moderate breeze. Skipper ashore. Time on passage from Cape Point Antonio 29 days. From Buenos Aires 32 days.
>
> Here endeth the passage.

9   The voyage of the 'Peri': Cape Town to London

Peri. Date and location of photo unknown.

We left Art as he arrived in Cape Town on January 29th, 1900. They stayed here until April 23rd; in that time they unloaded the cargo of South American grain, and refitted the ship to some extent. It had only taken them 32 days to sail the Atlantic from Buenos Aires; you sometimes get the impression that they sat around in port for longer than they were actually sailing!

As First Mate, Art was busy; on top of that there were clearly a number of other ships moored in the port, and he found quite a few people that he knew from previous voyages or school.

Sunday, February 4

> Began with gentle N'ly breeze and very fine clear weather. Took 4 boys in gig and sailed over to 'Mohawk' to see if I could discover any old faces. Found Languadock, chief, and Stapleton (who I was at school with, and who later on relieved me in the old 'Mohawk' when I left), second mate. Had a long yarn, but wouldn't stay to lunch, not being properly togged up, but arranged to return in afternoon. Did so, and had tea aboard, then went ashore with

> Stapes to the Cape Town Observatory to see Johns and Cochrane, two other old G.R.H.S's. Found them and spent the evening yarning. Got back to pier at 10.30 p.m., found it was blowing a living gale of wind. Waited till midnight and no boat coming, had to retrace our steps into town, and knocked up a friend of S's who kindly fixed us up with sleeping accommodations.
>
> <u>Monday, February 5</u>
>
> 5.30 a.m. turned out and made tracks for pier again. 7.0 a.m. 'Mohawk's' boat came off, and put me on board safely by 7.30 a.m. Gale gradually increasing during day. At 5.0 p.m. let go second anchor and 30 fathom, veering away to 75 fathom as starboard ditto. Hands employed variously, chipping over side, etc. Carpenter and 2 hands re-puttying poop seams.

The GRHS that he refers to is the 'Greenwich Royal Hospital School', which Art attended between the ages of 11 and 16. The 'Mohawk' is the steam ship in which he was Second Mate for voyages from London to New York in 1896-1897.

On Monday 12th February they still hadn't found a berth to begin unloading. There was still plenty of maintenance work on the ship to do, however.

> <u>Monday, February 12</u>
>
> Light airs or calm. Hands chipping and painting over side and deck ironwork, painting poop water ways and scraping jibboom. Put lifeboat in water, but being in bad condition, took her aboard on main deck for repairs. One A.B. deserted this day while ashore in boat with captain.

Someone came up with the bright idea of unloading some of the cargo into boats, to reduce the draught of the ship, and allow her to get into a berth. Art was not impressed!

> <u>Wednesday, February 14</u>
>
> Wind moderated at 8.0 a.m. Hove up port anchor, the same coming up foul; unshackled starb. cable to clear hawse. At 1.0 p.m. surf boats came off from S/S "Lulu Bohlen" with crowd of n******

> Commenced discharging cargo into them, the boats then being towed round to docks and discharged. Tommy rotten method this! The idea is to lighten ship, and try and get an earlier dock berth on the lighter draught. Won't work!

He was right; they went on doing this for a couple of days, but there was still no berth; eventually a steamer managed by the same agents was brought alongside, and grain was unloaded into her.

That was a lot faster; the steam ship presumably had powered winches, but it was still the 'Peri's crew that were doing the work.

Thursday, February 22

> Another A.B. deserted this evening while ashore in boat. Begins with light N'ly wind and fine clear weather. Resumed discharging at 6.0 a.m. and continued until 6.0 p.m., when the wind, having shifted to South, had increased to a fresh gale. "Lentwein" then left for dock with 140 tons yesterday. Let go second anchor in afternoon. The men complained of bread being weevily this day; found complaint to be just, so opened fresh lot. Had six hands from shore to assist with cargo this day; these had to stay on board all night on account of weather.

The crew are clearly not happy. They can't all go on shore, they are having to unload the cargo (140 tons is a lot), and the bread's got weevils in it. This is the second seaman who has deserted!

Over the next few days, the cargo was unloaded, ships stores, including coal and fresh water brought from the land, and, I suppose as a spin off from contact with the land, half of the crew, including Art, went down with the flu. On March 1st, the outside world made an appearance!

Thursday, March 1
> What ho! Ladysmith relieved! All Cape Town gone mad. Dead calm all morning, followed by moderate NW wind later. Hands chipping over side; boys scraping down. Carpenter repairing boat. Went ashore this morning and met Horace Dowling; brought him on board to dinner. Went ashore with him at 5.0 p.m., returning immediately. After tea, went ashore to see the jubilations. Had a very

"compressed" sort of time. Got aboard at 11.0 p.m.

The Boer war had at this stage been going on for five months, and Ladysmith, a town in Natal, had been besieged by the Boers. The war was to continue until 1902, by which time Art was back in the UK.
It sounds as if the Peri spent some time in dock, either for repairs or general maintenance, but there is no mention of a new cargo being loaded, so on the 23rd April, she was ready for the next stage of the voyage, to Timaru in New Zealand.

> Tuesday, April 24
>
> Wind increased rapidly after midnight, with a nasty sea. Reduced sail to topsails, courses, and heavy fore and afters. Weather fairly fine, but cloudy. Heavy sea at 8.0 a.m. The old girl has done more dancing about during the last 12 hours than she's done for many a long day. Wind and weather same to midnight. Stowed cables in lockers this day; fixed chafing gear, etc.
>
> Lat. 34° 59' S, Long. 16° 21' E.

With no cargo, the stability of the ship had to be ensured by loading ballast; rubble or whatever; anything to give enough weight at the bottom of the ship to give her stability. Of course, when you come to load the next cargo, all the ballast has to be shifted out of the hull again. Maybe they didn't load quite enough which would account for the 'Peri' 'dancing about'!

They are back in their old stamping ground of the Southern Ocean, and the weather is the same as ever; Art records three separate gales in the last week of April. But they are making progress; by April 30th, they have travelled 1000 miles from South Africa.

> Monday, April 30
>
> Steady strong wind increasing to moderate gale in morning. Weather fine and clear. All sail set; moderate following sea. The old girl fairly flying. This day at noon we completed the biggest day run we have yet done since leaving London, viz., 256 miles. There's life in the Peri yet. This day rendered doubly auspicious,

> it being the anniversary of the skipper's wife's birthday; kept as a holiday on board, the menu throughout the ship also being of special excellence, to celebrate the occasion. Cabin bill of fare included roast duck, champagne, coffee and cigars!! What ho! We bumped!!! Wind continued strong through night.
>
> Lat. 40° 10' S, Long. 35° 26' E.

I wonder where the duck came from? Were they a couple of unlucky ones that happened to fly past, or had they been living in the chicken coop since Cape Town? Either way, it's a step upwards from ship's bread with bugs crawling out of it!
The weather took no notice of the Skipper's wife's birthday!

Wednesday, May 2

> Light breeze came away at 1.0 a.m. from NE, hauling to North and gradually freshening, with continued thick rainy weather. Handed all light sail, and mainsail and topgallants later. Increased very rapidly in afternoon, with heavy rain and thunder squalls, and shifting to West. By 9.0 p.m. blowing a violent gale with a mountainous following sea. 10.0 p.m. all hands called (poor me below!) to furl upper topsails; succeeded after one solid hour's work. Forced to scud before it under foresail and upper topsails, heaving to being an impossibility. Steering very difficult, it taking two hands all their time at the wheel to prevent ship broaching to. Peri ran throughout like a duck, with dry decks. To illustrate the force of wind, at 11.0 p.m. during squall, our chicken pen - a solid construction of teak and iron kept on after bridge - blew clean into two parts, the halves hanging from the bridge by their respective lashings.
>
> Lat. 41° 37' S, Long. 42° 29' E.

This of course is the winter in the southern hemisphere, and the weather continued stormy. Quite apart from the difficulty of taking an accurate sighting of the sun from a ship that is pitching and rolling, when the sky is covered with cloud, or the horizon isn't clear, then no accurate sight is going to be possible. Those navigating have to rely on 'Dead Reckoning', or D.R, as Art refers to it. That means keeping as accurate as possible a record of both the direction travelled, and the speed of the ship.

Friday, May 18

Wind gradually westering and increasing to moderate breeze. Very fine weather with passing clouds and smooth sea. Set all drawable sail. Continued same throughout day, the wind remaining dead aft at W 1/2 S. Everything very settled in appearance. Hands working in 'tween decks all day. Night fine. Got sights this day - the first time for four days. Found compass error to have changed considerably from 2° W to 12° E, this putting ship well south of D.R. latitude. Longitude, however, almost exactly correct.

Lat. 44° 12' S, Long. 105° 50' E.

They have come a long way in the last 18 days; they are now 4500 miles from South Africa, and Australia is less than 1000 miles away to the North East.

Sunday, May 20

Today is dear little Queenie's birthday. Many very happy returns of the day Sis dear! Your Arty boy has been thinking of you all day. Wind steady from NW all day, with cloudy sky and passing misty patches of rain during morning. They have certainly got the better of us in the old country now as far as weather is concerned. Our nights are getting very long, cold and damp while those at home are getting correspondingly shorter and warmer. Wind freshening slightly towards midnight. Handed all light canvas. Passed Cape Leeuwin. Lat. 43° 56' S, Long. 113° 7' E.

'Queenie' was Art's sister; born in 1890, so eleven years old.

We've come across Cape Leewin before; the 'Peri' came here after leaving Fremantle in June the year before. Since then they have done a complete circumnavigation of the globe, via Buenos Aires and Cape Town. With the stops in those ports, it's taken them eleven months.

They have a patch of good weather, but then the winter re-asserts itself.

Sunday, June 3

Begins with strong wind steady from N by E all day with dense rainy fog first part, clearing in afternoon. Took in topgallants and light staysails at 5.0 a.m. and mainsail at 8.0 a.m. This is our third day now without sights and we are only 260 odd miles to the Snares! Hope we get a look at "Jamaica" tomorrow!! At 7.0 p.m. got good stellar observations, the sky clearing for an hour. Position 48° 40' S 161° 19' E. 8.0 p.m. wind increasing, handed upper topsail. Kept ship by the wind all night.

D.R. Lat. 48° 16' S, Long. 159° 51'

The meaning of 'Jamaica' has got lost in the last 120 years; they may be relying on dead reckoning, but they are in the wrong ocean for Jamaica! It's interesting here that Art lists both where he thought they were (DR) and where they actually turned out to be having got a good observation from the stars. A degree in longitude in this area is something in the region of 50 miles, so the difference between the estimate and the actual could be about 75 miles. As Art says, that could be critical when you are getting close to land. 'The Snares' are a group of uninhabited islands 125 miles to the south of the South Island of New Zealand.

Timaru, where they were headed, is about half way up the east coast of the South Island. As they got closer they were about to use lighthouses to fix their exact position.

Sunday, June 10

Just after midnight Morangi Lt. abeam 7 dist. At 2.0 a.m. brisk breeze came away from S'd, and continued. 4.15 a.m. Cape Wanbrow abeam. Hauled ship in shore at daylight, the wind falling lighter. Continued jogging along shore, until 2.0 p.m. arrived off Timaru. Clewed up all sail but topsails and hove to for pilot. 3.0 p.m. pilot and tug came off; proceeded into harbour, making fast at a buoy at 4.0 p.m., all Timaru being down on the wharf to watch our arrival, it being Sunday afternoon. Stowed all sail and tea-ho!! Here endeth another passage.

There are gaps in Art's diary here; they clearly spent some days getting the ballast out of the ship, then moved to a different wharf and loaded a cargo for London; but first they have to go to Lyttleton; still on South Island, but 150 miles up the coast. The 'Timaru Herald' records in 28th June 1900 that the 'Peri' was loading for London 'on account of the Canterbury Farmers Co-operative Association'

Wednesday, June 27

Completed the 600 tons cargo aboard preparatory to going to Lyttelton for dry docking, for repairs to rudder, as ordered by surveyor.

Ships then and now are kept to a certain standard of maintenance, allowing them and their cargos to be insured. Clearly the local surveyor wasn't happy with the condition of the rudder; Lyttleton had a dry dock which allowed work to be done. The opportunity was taken to 'scale and paint' in Art's words, the outside of the hull, and to check the accuracy of the compasses. Generally a 10,000 mile service; or rather a 37,000 mile service considering the distance the 'Peri' had travelled since they left London. While they were there they also loaded wool and tallow. They were back in Timaru on July 28th, finishing loading and securing cargo. They were ready to leave; but it wasn't straightforward.

Wednesday, August 15

Tug came off at 7.0 a.m. Unmoored from buoy; while getting tow rope aboard, the tug got it foul of propeller. 9.30 a.m. got spring clear, but in the interval C. Lindskog A.B., being very bad apparently with erysipelas, sent for doctor. He immediately ordered him to hospital. 3.0 p.m. before skipper got back. We are thus leaving, two men short, the carpenter having deserted last week. Very light N'ly airs and fine clear weather. At 3.30 p.m. Capt. Clarkson came off with tug. 4.0 p.m. unmoored and proceeded to sea. Goodbye Timaru. Very sorry to leave you! 4.30 p.m. set topsails. 5.0 p.m. let go tug, pilot leaving also. Timaru Lt. bearing W 1/2 N 5 miles. Set all plain sail. Managed to hold a light N'ly wind all night to claw off with. 11.15 p.m. Timaru light dipped.

On 21st August, the 11th day out, Art records that it was exactly 21 months since they had left London. The winds were light, and he doesn't hold out much hope of getting home for Christmas. For the first time he records the skipper being laid up with 'rheumatic gout', which is going to be a recurring story for the next couple of months.

Saturday, September 1, 1900

Another month commenced. How the time does skip! Continued blowing a fresh gale greater part of day, with cloudy weather and heavy rain squalls at times. Very heavy sea: "Peri," however, behaving simply splendidly, riding everything like a duck. There's no mistake, she's in splendid trim. In afternoon, weather breaking and gale moderating somewhat. Set fore topsail and kept away to course. P.M. gradually set all plain sail. Wind remaining steady fresh from North. Weather overcast and windy looking.

Lat. 49° 26' S, Long. 145° 46' W.

Whoever it was who had been responsible for loading the cargo had clearly got it exactly right; maybe the maintenance work to the ship had helped. This position puts them 2000 miles from New Zealand, with another 3000 to go to Cape Horn. However on 13th September they sighted another ship, the 'Aberfoyle' which had left Timaru 11 days after them. Art was not pleased! He cheered up a couple of days later when he worked out that they had sailed 1270 miles in the last week, or an average of 181 per day. 'This is first class going'!

Monday, September 17 - 34th day

Begins with fresh breeze, gradually increasing to a moderate gale by 10.0 a.m. with heavy snow squalls; heavy following sea. Ship rolling pretty lively and shipping some water, but running well withal. Furled fore topgallants. At 2.0 p.m. heavy snow storm passed over - continuing to 4.0 p.m., settling heavily. The ship presenting a typical wintry appearance by 4.0 p.m.; yards, masts, etc., being well coated. Fine clear weather ensuing, soon made a change, bunging decks up with slush. Another good day's run today; would certainly have had to heave to had we been timber laden. Only about 480 miles to Di-

-ego Ramirez Islands at noon today. Latter part of day, strong breeze with heavy snow squalls, but fine generally. Set main topgallants. Wind W by N. Lat. 55° 50' S, Long. 82° 53' W.

The Diego Ramirez Islands are about 60 miles to the south of Cape Horn. On the 19th, they sighted the Islands; pretty much where Art expected them to be. He was very pleased with himself:

> navigating the ship for three weeks now, the old man not interfering in the slightest. In fact he worries about nothing but his pains, the whole of which have now concentrated themselves in the right thigh.

They passed Cape Horn; they passed the Falkland Islands on the 24th; the skipper continued to be ill! In fact, Art is beginning to see a link between the skipper and the weather…..

Sunday, September 30

The last day of September! Another month gone!! Where does the time go to. The day began with a moderate gale from the Nor'd with dirty gloomy weather and heavy rain. The two latter items have continued throughout the day without intermission, although the wind moderated greatly up to 8.0 a.m. and has continued so, but coming in the shape of squalls in afternoon. I wonder when this wind is going to shift. I suppose it's a case now; the old man has managed to put his head on deck for 3 consecutive days now, for an average of four minutes, and I reckon this accounts for the whole lot of this head wind we're having. He's the Jonah on board this ship safe enough. Towards night fell dead calm, with sky overcast and thick misty weather. Glass falling.

By D.R. Lat. 44° 39' S, Long. 46° 52' W.

They seem to be stuck in the South Atlantic. They badly need winds that will allow them to sail northwards. Things do improve; by October 7th, they are at latitude 34 degrees, and by Friday October 12th at latitude 27 degrees south. The wind is not doing what it's supposed to do, however:

> Wind is steady between E and ENE. Cannot understand this wind at all; we have had it now from the same direction since last Monday

and the prospects this evening are just exactly the same as they were then. It is hardly possible that they are the trades, but whatever they are, we cannot stand on this tack much longer or we shall be in Brazil. The prevailing winds here are supposed to be, and generally are, NW-N-NNE. Bad luck! The old man had better lay up again I think!!

Finally things improve. The position on the 21st puts them roughly level with Rio di Janeiro.

> Sunday, October 21 - 68th day
>
> Got the SE Trades. Gentle WSW-SW-S-SE wind all day with very fine clear weather and smooth sea. This has been our first very hot day. All sail set. Wind gradually increasing to a fine fresh breeze in the evening. The London girls seem to have got hold of the tow-rope at last! If we can only get across the Line before the 4th or 5th of next month, our chances of Xmas home will again look rosy!!
>
> Lat. 21° 13' S, Long. 25° 58' W.

On October 28th, they crossed the Equator. The 'Peri' was not the fastest of ships; on November 5th, when they were at Latitude 16 degrees North (level with the Caribbean), Art records that they

> 'Passed a barque - wooden box - rolling down for the West Indies, her course lying at right angles to our own; think it necessary to mention this, to account for the fact aforementioned that we "passed" her.'

This must be the section in Art's diaries with the fewest gales mentioned; in fact all the way through to 22nd November, it's almost perfect sailing weather. They are now at Latitude 46 degrees north, Longitude 16 west, which puts them close to Spain.

> Sunday, November 25
>
> Just two years today since we left the London docks on this ever memorable voyage. Where on earth has the time gone, and yet somehow I often wonder whether I ever was in England, as it might just as well have been five years as two. I cannot realize in the

least that we are so near home as is really the case. At 4.0 a.m. this morning watch I was greatly aided in realizing the true state of affairs, however, by seeing the loom of the Lizard Lights before the port beam. 6.0 a.m. Lizard Lts. abeam, 25 miles distant. Shaped a course for Start Pt. Wind strong with brisk rain squalls; furled Main topgallants. Got pennant and fish tackle aloft and put anchors on the rail. During day weather fining up and wind moderating. Shook out reefs and set all sail in afternoon. 1:45 p.m. Start Pt. abeam, distant 6 miles.

So they did make it home for Christmas; in fact with a whole month to spare! This was the last of Art's long voyages; we suspect that he left the 'Peri' in London with the desire of never seeing her or the Skipper ever again!

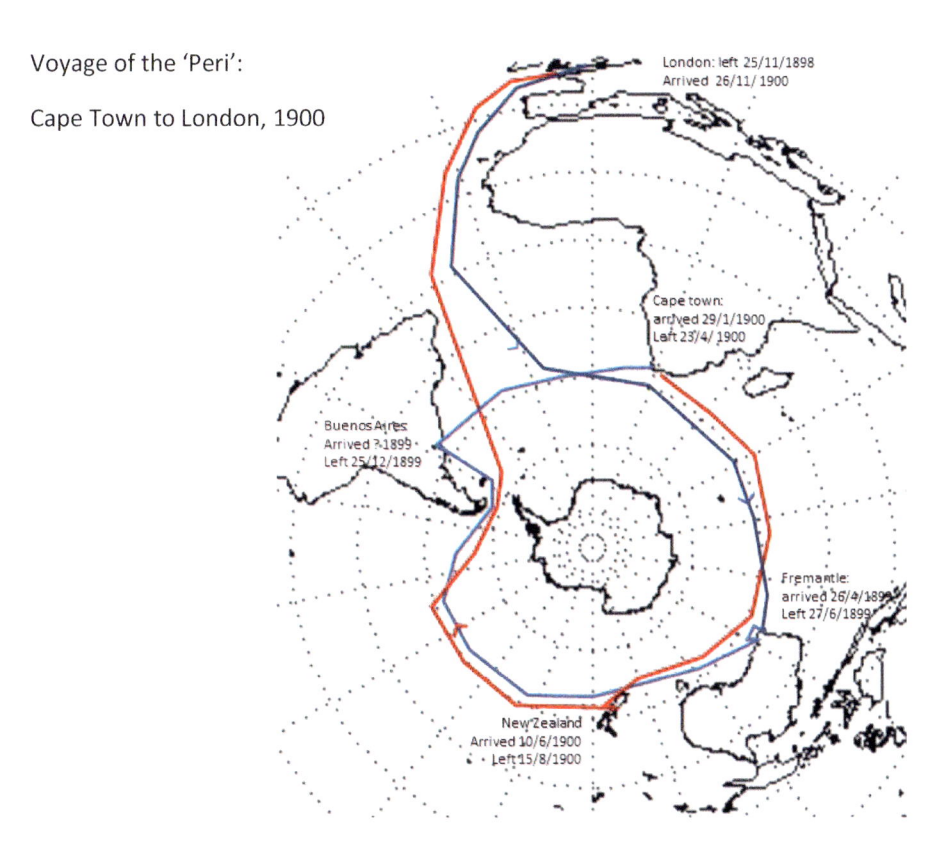

Voyage of the 'Peri':

Cape Town to London, 1900

10   Closer to home.

This is now November 1900; it's the very last months of the Victorian era. Art has accumulated a grand total of just over 8 years and 1 month of time at sea, in 6 different ships, ranging in size from a Thames paddle steamer to a wool clipper. He's been around the world five times, and to America five times; that really ought to be enough experience to qualify him to do almost anything at sea.

It is certainly enough to get him his Master's certificate, which is awarded on the 30th January 1901, and having sat an examination on the 16th March, his 'Extra Master's certificate' on the 18th March. We suspect that he had spent a couple of months cramming on the knowledge needed to pass the exams; in his papers is a postcard from 'Broughtons Nautical Academy, Watling Street, London'.

Is it enough to get him the coveted licence as a Thames River pilot? Maybe not. His next job is back on the paddle steamers again; he is taken on as First Mate of the Royal Sovereign in May, probably when the season started. You will remember that Art had been the 2nd Mate in the same ship some four years before, in the summer of 1896.

Royal Sovereign, with funnels lowered to pass under London Bridge.

He is certainly more experienced now, and might well be concentrating a bit more; part of the requirement of being a Pilot is having a detailed knowledge of the navigation of the River Thames. Taking a paddle steamer loaded with passengers up and down it every day, in all weathers and at all stages of the tide would have been as good a way of amassing that knowledge as any.

That job lasts until the autumn, at the beginning of September. He has a couple of weeks at home, then becomes the First Mate in a steamship called the 'Sea Hound', owned by a company called 'Leach & Co' who advertised 'regular sailings between London and Ghent', which is in Belgium. It's difficult to know whether they sailed all the way to Ghent, which is some way inland from the coast but with a canal connection to the sea, or whether there was a rail connection for the last leg of the journey.

The Sea Hound was one of four ships owned by Leach & Co; she was 228 ft long, and must have been pretty much brand new; the records show that she had been built in Govan, on the River Clyde, and completed in 1901. She appears to have been designed for steady carrying of cargo and passengers, rather than for speed; Art might be either amused or shocked by her modern equivalent, the ferry 'Pride of Hull' which is over 600 ft long, and does the rather longer journey from Hull to Rotterdam in 12 hours flat.

There is actually a link between the two ships; Leach & Co was taken over by the 'General Steam Navigation Company' in 1919, and they in turn were taken over by P & O Steam Navigation in 1920; and they are the owners and operators of the 'Pride of Hull'!

His work on the 'Sea Hound' lasts until the beginning of March 1902, when he moves smartly across the quay to become First Mate on her sister ship, the 'Sea Gull'. She must have been pretty much the same design; built a couple of years earlier in the same shipyard on the Clyde. The difference is that instead of just shuttling to and fro across the Channel, the Sea Gull is trading to Morocco and the Canary Islands as well. In August that year, Art is promoted; he is now the Master of the Sea Gull. All that hard work has paid off; one hopes that he now gets the money to go with the responsibility. He does another short stint back in the 'Sea Hound' from January to

March 1903, and then waves goodbye to the company. It looks as if he has accumulated 10 years of sea time; and that suggests that that is the magic amount needed to apply for a pilot's license.

In Art's papers, (and we are not surprised that he kept this) is a letter from the Trinity House, who license Pilots, dated 25th March 1903. 'You are requested to attend with certificates of qualifications obtained……'

On May 23rd, his diary records that he went down to Gravesend, which is where he would be based as a Pilot 'for a preliminary canter'. He takes charge of his first ship, the SS Hermes, sailing from London to Blythe in Northumberland, on the 6th June 1903. He is Thames pilot No 1501, at the age of 26.

So that's his professional life; what's happened at home? We told you that when he sailed on board the 'Peri', at the end of 1898, he was clearly very attached to 'Flo'; there are numerous entries in his diaries saying how much he was missing her. You will remember that she was the daughter of the Organist at the chapel that both families attended in Greenwich.

The story in the family is that when he arrived at Fremantle, in April 1899, he met another young lady, name of Laura. Suddenly there is no mention in his diaries of Flo anymore; or at least not until he gets to Cape Town at the end of January 1900, when there are two letters from her waiting for him.

The story is that he politely asked Flo if their engagement (if that is what it was) could be broken off; the answer was a firm NO, as much from her parents as from her. In those days a young man could be sued for 'breach of promise', and a young lady who had been betrothed and then jilted was spoiled goods; imagine the embarrassment, especially in the Chapel!

It's reading between the lines at 100+ years distance, but we suspect that Art accepted the situation. He had only known Laura for a maximum of two months, after all; did he write her letters? We don't know.

Once he is home, in 1901, he presumably starts seeing Flo again, and, with his professional prospects looking good, a wedding is arranged, for July 1903. One fine day, there is a knock at the door of the Owen family residence in Greenwich. Two young ladies and their father stand on the step. Hello, says one, in a strong Australian accent; I'm Laura, Art's fiancé!

Consternation! It actually got worse, if that were possible; the other young lady was Bessie, Laura's sister, and she was attracted to Art's brother Ernest!

The family story is that the night before the wedding, Laura and Art sat in the house's conservatory, weeping into each other's arms. The story may have got embroidered a bit along the way; Art describes the wedding in his diary.

> Saturday, July 25 1903
>
> Our wedding day! Married at 2.30 p.m. at May Hill Church by Rev. R.S. Jones. Weather beautifully fine. Reception afterwards at Helensdale - great success in every way. 4.45 p.m. Flo and I left for Eastbourne via Greenwich and L. Bridge (L.B & P.C), after visiting Crown Hill to shake out confetti. Arrived at Eastbourne about 8.30 p.m. Got comfortable diggings ten minutes later.

That doesn't sound like the thoughts of a man who had spent the previous night sobbing in the arms of another woman, even if he thought there was a chance his diary might be read by his new wife.

Wedding of Arthur Owen and Florence Batchelor, July 1903

The author, for very personal reasons, is glad that the wedding did go ahead; Art and Flo were married for 54 years and had four children, one of whom was my father!

Art's sister, Queenie, apparently did stay in touch with Laura, and the good news is that both she and Bessie met and married nice Australian men. Incidentally one person who was definitely not happy at the time of the wedding was Queenie, sitting far left in the photograph. She had suffered from Polio as a child, and as a result had to wear a brace and a boot. Because she wasn't old enough to have 'come out' she was not allowed to wear a long skirt, which meant that she was embarrassed by her brace. She tried to hide it with the trailing flowers of her bouquet!

We started this account talking about the £30 that Art's father invested in his son's apprenticeship. Was the cunning plan to give his son a well paid steady job, a success? Yes. Art has left a note of what he earned in his first six months as a River Pilot; £90. It doesn't sound much, but the average annual income in Britain in 1900 was £42; so on an annual basis Art was on four times that. Working out what a given amount of money was worth is difficult, but sources on the web suggests that £180 a year in 1903 is equivalent to £25,000 a year in 2021; not a bad starting salary for a 26 year old. It was certainly enough to get married and (the next year) to buy a house in Gravesend, close to 'the office'. When our father was born (their second child), four years later, the family had a servant and the baby had a nursemaid; comfortably middle class!

So did Art and Flo live happily ever after? As far as we know, yes; they stayed in Gravesend, and Art continued to work as a pilot until his retirement. Pilotage would have been a 'reserved occupation' in the First World War, so his work continued through that conflict. While pilots generally worked on a 'Hobson's choice' basis; (the pilot who had been waiting the longest took the next ship that needed a pilot, however big or small the ship was), Art became the 'pilot of choice' for the 'Union Castle' line, whose London base was at Tilbury, just across the river from Gravesend.

The only tragedy in their married lives that we know about was the death of their youngest son. Born in 1916, Douglas got a job in a bank, and joined the Territorial Army; he was called up by the Royal Engineers just before the outbreak of the Second World War. He lost his life in the sinking of H M Transport 'Lancastria' in the aftermath of Dunkirk. The pain of that loss to his parents is evident in the entry in the family Bible made by his father.

Our father was born in 1907; he badly wanted to go to sea, just like his father and grandfather, but Art absolutely refused to allow him to do that. It wasn't until he was 21 and had some freedom in the matter that my Dad trained as a wireless telegraphist; but by the time he finished that, it was the Depression, and there were no ships! He did satisfy some of the genetic urge to go to sea by joining the RNVR before the Second World war, and served, using his training as an electrical engineer, in the UK, Ceylon and East Africa.

Art continued working until 1938; Flo died in 1957, and he followed her a year later at the age of 81.

Art and Flo in 1949

The London Pilot

Print of etching by Norman Wilkinson

Appendix 1:   Sources for illustrations

1. Four Brothers from family collection
2. Prize giving certificate 1892. Family collection
3. Sail Plan of Mermerus: from Macgregor D.R. 1988. 'Fast Sailing Ships' Conway 1988
4. Four Apprentices from family collection
5. Mermerus in Melbourne. Postcard in family collection.
6. 'Moshulu' in the South Atlantic. From Newby, E. 'Learning the ropes'. Times Books 1999.
7. Mermerus in Melbourne from Lubbock, B. 'The Colonial Clippers' Brown & Son, Glasgow 1924, annotated by ANO.
8. East India Docks, London c.1888 Pinterest JerelynH and
    The Wool Fleet 1890 from painting by Maurice Randall. Family collection.
9. In the Doldrums: Painting by AJA Owen. Family collection
10. Art Owen on board Mermerus 1895. Family collection
11. Mermerus under full sail. Painting by Spurling, copied from magazine cover.
12. Koh-i-Noor. Postcard from collection of Mick Twyman
13. Four generations; family collection.
14. Model of 'La Marguerite' in Liverpool Museum. Copied from photo in Guardian newspaper.
15. Copy of Board of Trade experience certificate. Family collection
16. Model of the brig 'Messenger' made by ANO. Family collection.
17. 'Wearing a Ship' from Villiers, A. 'The Way of a Ship' Scribners 1970.
18. Barque Peri. Collection of South Australia State Library, ref 1373/7/52
19. Photo of Art taken in Fremantle, June 1899. Family collection
20. Crew of the 'Peri'. Family collection.
21. Barque Peri. Collection of South Australia State Library, ref 1373/7/53
22. Royal Sovereign Paddle Steamer; postcard in family collection.
23. Wedding of Art Owen and Florence Batchelor, July 1903. Family collection.
24. Art and Flo in 1949. Family collection.
25. The London Pilot. Print of an etching by Norman Wilkinson. Family collection

World maps:. Information from AR Owen's diaries; base plan Polar Azimuthal projection from climsurv.ipsl.polytechnique.fr

Appendix 2: Further reading

I have leaned heavily on five books for background information and guidance, and am happy to acknowledge the expertise of their authors. In no particular order they are:

1. LUBBOCK, Basil: The Colonial Clippers. Brown & Son, Glasgow, 1924
2. VILLIERS, Alan: The Way of a Ship. Scribners, New York 1970
3. VILLIERS, Alan: Square-Rigged Ships, An Introduction. National Maritime Museum, London.
4. GREENHILL, Basil: The life and death of the Merchant Sailing Ship. National Maritime Museum, London 1980.
5. NEWBY, Eric. Learning the Ropes. Times Books 1999.

If you have an academic interest in the records of A N Owen's voyages, please contact the author.

Appendix 3: Glossary

Barque: a sailing ship with three masts, with square sails only on the front two masts.

Box hauled: If the conditions are too rough to allow the ship to be tacked, the ship is allowed to go backwards, and the rudder is used to bring the ship around to the new direction of travel.

Broaching: to allow the ship to swing so that the wind is blowing into the side of the ship; very dangerous.

Courses: the biggest, lowest sails on each mast.

Crojack: the yard used to secure the lower corners of the mizzen topsail. It would have been unusual to set a square sail (course) on this yard because it would have interfered with the 'Spanker'; see below.

Dog watch: a work shift, splitting one of the normal four hour watches in half. Necessary to stop the same group of sailors standing the watch which falls in the middle of every night

Downhaul: a rope applying a downward force on a spar or sail.

Gaskets: the ropes used to secure a furled sail to the yard.

Gilguy; either a rope temporarily used as a guy, or simply some sort of gadget!

Heave to: in stormy weather, to head the ship into the wind, and, with her bows to the oncoming seas, let her drift.

Jib: a triangular sail set between the bowsprit and the foremast.

Jibboom: a spar which forms a forward extension of the bowspirit.

Poop: the raised deck at the stern of the ship.

Port tack 'Port' is the left hand side of the ship; being on the 'Port Tack' is therefore sailing with the wind coming from the port side.

Reefed topsail: the depth of the sail is reduced to reduce the area exposed to the wind.

Royal yard/sail: the square sail above the upper topgallant.

Sennit: braided cordage used to make mats or lashings.

Spanker: the fore and aft sail set on the lower section of the mizzen mast.

Staysail: a triangular sail set between one mast and the next.

Throat seizings; binding together the ends of a looped rope.

Trysail: a storm sail set to the rear of the main mast in place of the main course.

Printed in Great Britain
by Amazon